KYLE BUSCH

SPORTS STARS
who give back

GIFTED AND GIVING RACING STAR

by Ryan Basen

Enslow Publishers, Inc.
40 Industrial Road
Box 398
Berkeley Heights, NJ 07922
USA
http://www.enslow.com

Library of Congress Cataloging-in-Publication Data
Basen, Ryan.
  Kyle Busch : gifted and giving racing star / Ryan Basen.
      p. cm. — (Sports stars who give back)
  Includes bibliographical references and index.
  Summary: "A biography of American NASCAR driver Kyle Busch, focusing on his philanthropic activities off the track"—Provided by publisher.
  ISBN 978-0-7660-3589-8
  1. Busch, Kyle—Juvenile literature. 2. Automobile racing drivers—United States—Biography—Juvenile literature. 3. Philanthropists—United States—Biography—Juvenile literature. I. Title.
  GV1032.B89B37 2010
  796.72092—dc22
  [B]
                                    2009026185

Printed in the United States of America

102009 Lake Book Manufacturing, Inc., Melrose Park, IL

10 9 8 7 6 5 4 3 2 1

To Our Readers: We have done our best to make sure all Internet addresses in this book were active and appropriate when we went to press. However, the author and the publisher have no control over and assume no liability for the material available on those Internet sites or on other Web sites they may link to. Any comments or suggestions can be sent by e-mail to comments@enslow.com or to the address on the back cover.

♻ Enslow Publishers, Inc. is committed to printing our books on recycled paper. The paper in every book contains between 10% to 30% post-consumer waste (PCW). The cover board on the outside of each book contains 100% PCW. Our goal is to do our part to help young people and the environment too!

Photo credits: John Raoux/AP Images, 1; Russ Hamilton/AP Images, 8; Mary Ann Chastain/AP Images, 10; Jae C. Hong/AP Images, 16, 53; Tony Gutierrez/AP Images, 18, 106; Chris Gardner/AP Images, 22, 69; Terry Renna/AP Images, 29, 47; Joe Cavaretta/AP Images, 31; Rusty Burroughs/AP Images, 36; Carlos Osorio/AP Images, 38, 80; Chris O'Meara/AP Images, 43; Matt Sayles/AP Images, 58, 96; Glenn Smith/AP Images, 62; Steve Helber/AP Images, 67; John Russell/AP Images, 77; Diane Bondareff/AP Images, 88; Keith Shimada/AP Images, 94; Rainier Ehrhardt/AP Images, 102

Cover Photo: John Raoux/AP Images

CONTENTS

BREAKOUT

Kyle Busch was eager. It was August 10, 2008, and the twenty-three-year-old NASCAR driver was leading the Centurion Boats at The Glen, a Sprint Cup Series race in New York.

Suddenly, with only eight laps remaining, a multi-car accident paused the action. Busch was not involved in the wreck, but the race was suspended for nearly forty-five minutes.

Busch, along with 87,000 fans at Watkins Glen International, patiently awaited the restart. The young driver had led for the previous twenty laps of the ninety-lap race. Now he was barely in front of Tony Stewart, one of the top drivers on the Sprint Cup circuit.

"I was a little nervous having Tony behind us and sitting there for so long," Busch said later. "I wondered if we were going to have a flat spot on the tires. I wondered what we were going to do, how we were going to get good on the restart, when I was going to turn the brake fans on and what would I do if I get down in Turn One and somebody gets alongside you."[1]

But he would wonder no more. Busch calmed his nerves. After a great restart, he outlasted Stewart to the checkered flag, finishing two seconds ahead of Stewart for the win.

It was a landmark victory for Busch, one of many he enjoyed in 2008. In the Sprint Cup, NASCAR's top racing series, Busch had won four of the past seven races and eight overall. The win also clinched a berth in the Chase for the Sprint Cup, a ten-race competition at the end of the season that determines the Sprint Cup champion.

Busch won a combined twenty-one races in NASCAR's three series: The Sprint Cup,

DID YOU KNOW?

Kyle's hobbies include surfing, hanging out with his terriers Kelly and Suzie, and cheering on the Denver Broncos.

Nationwide, and Craftsman Truck circuits. Busch also set a record by becoming the first driver to win on three road courses during a season.

And it was only his fourth full season competing at the top level. In his first season with Joe Gibbs Racing, Busch emerged as one of NASCAR's superstars and perhaps even its top driver.

"This year has just been phenomenal," Busch said after the Glen victory. "It's just crazy."[2]

A CHOSEN ONE

Busch's success was not necessarily a surprise. He grew up in an enthusiastic racing family, and older brother Kurt Busch also reached a high level. Kurt won a Nextel Cup title in 2004 (it became the Sprint Cup in 2008).

As kids, the Busch brothers were obsessed with racing. They learned about strategy, the insides of cars, and how to win at early ages. They quickly became competitive, assertive drivers—qualities they are still known for today.

"I just hate to lose," Kyle Busch said. "I love winning. That's what I am all about. I guess people don't like me for getting as upset as I am sometimes when I lose, but that's me."[3]

Kyle wasted no time applying the skills he had learned growing up. He won numerous amateur races as a kid. When Kurt reached NASCAR's top series, Kyle's success as a teenager also received national attention.

Kyle drove in the Craftsman Truck Series as a sixteen-year-old and drove full-time on the Busch circuit (later renamed the Nationwide Series) at nineteen. He even won five races during his rookie season on the Busch Series in 2004.

As a twenty-year-old, Kyle joined the Sprint Cup Series full-time. He was immediately a driver to reckon with. He won a race in his first full season, 2005, and qualified for the Chase the following season (only twelve of the forty-three full-time drivers on the Cup series qualify for the Chase). He made the Chase again in 2007.

KYLE'S CAR

Sponsor: M&M's
Car Manufacturer: Toyota
Car No.: 18
Car Owner: Joe Gibbs
Team: Joe Gibbs Racing
Crew Chief: Steve Addington

Busch celebrates his victory at the Centurion Boats at The Glen race in 2008.

"He looked like he'd been doing it for fifteen years," veteran driver Mark Martin said of Busch's early Cup career.[4]

But none of those seasons could compare with 2008. Kyle won eight Sprint Cup races, second only to Carl Edwards's nine. He also became the first driver to compete in three NASCAR races on three different tracks in the same weekend. His ten wins on the Nationwide Series tied a record, and he also won three races on the truck series.

"I can't remember when a driver has been so successful across the board in three series simultaneously," said Barry Schmoyer, president of the Driver of the Year Foundation.[5]

"Man, that was pretty phenomenal," Busch said. "I don't know if I could ever do it again, but to be accustomed to winning this year hasn't really sunk in."[6]

Kyle made a splash by winning so much early in his career, but he also matured as a driver and grew up as a person. He entered NASCAR as a fiery, immature, aggressive driver. He is still aggressive and sometimes hot-headed, but he is learning how to work better with teammates and race more cleanly. That bodes well for the future.

"If Kyle can manage his aggressiveness, I don't think anybody can touch him," driver Jeff Gordon said. "Kyle is a tremendous talent and just constantly shows it over and over again. But I think there is still a learning process to go through there in patience and maturity for him and that team."[7]

> **"If Kyle can manage his aggressiveness, I don't think anybody can touch him."**
>
> —Jeff Gordon

A CONTROVERSIAL FIGURE

Kyle is one of the most controversial drivers in NASCAR. Many fans and teammates love him for his ability to win and his straightforward personality. Some fans and drivers detest Kyle, though. It has not been uncommon for fans to boo Kyle after he wins.

They do not like him because his rival is the popular driver Dale Earnhardt, Jr. And, Kyle's brother Kurt is also known to have a fiery personality.

Busch prepares to race at the 2009 Food City 500 in Bristol, Tennessee.

Kyle has developed a reputation as one of NASCAR's "bad guys," which is a bit of a compliment. It does not mean he is a bad person.

Some drivers resent that Kyle causes wrecks and say he does not race with class. It might also hurt his popularity with other drivers that he wins so often. Either way, he is respected on the track.

"He's driving his heart out, and it's working," said Buddy Baker, who, like Busch, was known for being an aggressive driver when he competed in NASCAR in the 1970s and '80s. "It'll tick some guys off, but not many guys have been that good.

DID YOU KNOW?

Kyle has his own clothing line called Rowdy Style.

Like him or not, he's at a place in the sport that had to be filled."[8]

Busch is also a caring person. He runs a foundation to help underprivileged kids and also volunteers his time to assist charities run by other NASCAR drivers.

Love him or hate him, everyone agrees that Kyle Busch is a rising star in NASCAR.

"Busch gets into a race car. And everybody watches," the *Charlotte Observer* wrote. "Ask the folks who know the sport which driver has the most talent and for years you heard Jeff Gordon or [Tony] Stewart. Now? You hear Busch."[9]

The August 2008 win at Watkins Glen confirmed Busch's emergence, as did many other races that year. He relied on his confidence, cunning, and tremendous driving ability to win those races. Those attributes were born while growing up in Las Vegas, Nevada.

DID YOU KNOW?

Kyle's favorite restaurants include In-N-Out Burger and Baja Fresh.

2

GROWING UP ON WHEELS

Kyle Busch made his debut on NASCAR's elite Nextel Cup Series in 2004, when he was only nineteen. His brother Kurt Busch had started racing on the Cup circuit a few years earlier, when Kurt was just twenty-two. The average age of Cup series drivers at the time was much higher: thirty-seven.

Whether or not they knew it, the Busch brothers spent much of their childhood developing sophisticated racing skills. Their upbringing no doubt helped them break into the elite series so early. Kyle and Kurt are the only children of Tom and Gaye Busch. Their parents were middle-class working professionals in Las Vegas, Nevada. Gaye worked for the Clark County school system for thirty years. Tom was an auto mechanic.

LAS VEGAS, NEVADA

Population: 553,000

Location: Southwest Nevada, near the California border

Known for: Casinos, shows, and amusement parks

Las Vegas is a popular tourist town famous for its casinos, amusement parks, and live performances. It is not a city known for having roots in elite stock car racing. Most top drivers come from elsewhere, especially the southeastern United States, which is more than 1,000 miles (1,609 km) from Las Vegas.

But the Busch family was different from most Las Vegas natives. Tom was an avid racer and competed in dozens of short track races all around Nevada. He won more than fifty races overall. He even built a fourteen-stall garage behind the family's home where he could work on the vehicles. Tom's hobby would rub off on his sons. The Busch boys sometimes went bowling or to hang out at Gameworks, a huge video arcade. But most of the time they were either in school or racing.

Kyle's daily routine as a kid usually included: "Go to school, go home, work on racecars, play with (remote control) cars, whatever it entailed. And then the weekend stuff was always going out to the racetrack. That's pretty much where I lived."[1]

Despite their intense racing hobby, Kyle and Kurt did not miss out on much. "In our neighborhood there really weren't any other kids for Kurt and Kyle to play with," Tom said, "so they spent almost all of their time working on the cars."[2]

PUSHED BY KURT

Kyle benefited from spending time around cars with his father. He also gained from having a competitive older brother.

Kurt and Kyle sometimes raced go-karts in the cul-de-sac they grew up on. Kurt usually won. One time when Kyle was seven, though, Kurt was coasting during a cul-de-sac race. He let his little brother take an early lead. But Kurt did not want to lose, so he passed Kyle late in the race. Kyle was desperate to win, but he realized there wasn't much time. Near the end of the race, Kyle climbed over Kurt's left-rear tire and knocked the carburetor off. While Kurt sat there, Kyle passed him and won the race.

"It was like, in my mind, I had won the race because he had just clobbered me and wrecked me and took the power out of my car," Kurt recalled.

Kyle disagreed.

"You know what? I got back to the start/finish line first, so I won," he replied.[3]

Already at such a young age, Kyle's competitive desire was so strong that he would do almost anything to win. Part of that desire came from wanting to beat his older brother.

"I always wanted to be better than him," Kyle said, "but I always learned from him too. I went after the same things he did."[4]

Kyle and Kurt raced dwarf cars at the tiny Pahrump Valley Speedway, a dirt oval track in western Nevada. They also raced legends cars at the Bullring, an asphalt track next to the Las Vegas Motor Speedway. The Speedway hosts major NASCAR races every year.

When Kurt was a teenager, Tom and Kyle essentially became his teammates. They would go with Kurt to the track. Young Kyle would act as his brother's spotter and videotape the action. Sometimes he would be the crew chief. Afterward, all three sat down and reviewed the races. They analyzed what Kurt had done right and wrong and how the winner had taken the race. They also spent hours putting together cars.

LAS VEGAS MOTOR SPEEDWAY

Location: **Las Vegas, Nevada**

Size: **1.5 miles (2.4 km)**

Capacity crowd: **137,000**

Shape: **D-shaped oval**

Races: **Shelby 427, a NASCAR Sprint Cup race, every March; Sam's Town 300, a NASCAR Nationwide Series race, the day before the Shelby 427; Qwik Liner Las Vegas 350, a NASCAR Craftsman Truck race, every September**

Web site: **www.lvms.com**

Kurt (left) and Kyle Busch talk before a race in 2009.

"Kyle definitely has got the coach's son syndrome," said Alan Gustafson, who was Kyle's crew chief with Hendrick Motorsports from 2004–2007. "He's been subjected to the Xs and Os of the sport since Day One."[5]

A BUDDING RACING CAREER

When Kyle became a teenager, he started driving in legends and late-model stock car races. He won sixty-five races in legends cars from 1999–2001, including two track championships at the Bullring. He won ten late model races at the Bullring in 2001.

At sixteen he moved on full-time to the American Speed Association (ASA) circuit, a competitive series full of veteran drivers. This established a pattern: Every year Kyle won a lot of races. And every year he improved enough as a driver to move up to another circuit. Then he won some more. This trend would continue until Kyle landed on NASCAR's Cup series and could not go any further.

Sometimes the Buschs had to be creative to help Kyle pursue his racing career. When Kyle was fifteen, his father made up a phony birth certificate saying Kyle was sixteen so he could move up from legends cars to the late-model cars.

"My mom didn't like the idea, but she was OK with it," Kyle recalled. "My dad and I were all about it. So we did it."[6]

Around this time, Kurt was beginning to attract attention from NASCAR teams. He signed with Roush Racing in 1999 and began racing in the Craftsman Truck Series. He was tabbed to ascend to the Cup series within a year or two and touted as a future NASCAR star.

Kyle was still a few years away from graduating high school. He was not even old enough to get a

ROUSH FENWAY RACING

- Formerly Roush Racing, 1984–2007
- First Winston Cup Series driver: Mark Martin, 1988
- Employed Kurt Busch as driver, 1999–2005
- Based: Concord and Mooresville, North Carolina
- Web site: www.roushfenway.com

Kyle signs an autograph after winning the pole position at the O'Reilly 300 in 2004.

driver's license. But Kurt told anybody who would listen that if they thought Kurt was going to be a great driver, they should watch Kyle.

The Busch family was excited. It appeared that Kyle and Kurt were going to realize their dreams of competing against the top stock car drivers in the world. "Everyone always said they had talent, but we never believed it would be anything this big," Gaye Busch said.[7]

Pretty soon NASCAR teams were watching young Kyle. It would not be long before he followed Kurt into the sport.

GETTING STARTED

It was a late-summer day in Chicago, Illinois. In a week or two Kyle Busch would return to Durango High School in Las Vegas to start another school year. He made sure to enjoy the end of his summer break.

On that day, August 18, 2001, Busch raced in the Sears Craftsman 175 championship. The race was on NASCAR's Craftsman Truck Series at Chicago Motor Speedway. The sixteen-year-old competed against pro drivers much older and more experienced than him. That did not faze Kyle. He was in the top five for most of the race and led for seventeen laps toward the end.

Then, in the 165th lap, Kyle's Eldon Ford truck ran out of gas, costing him a chance to win the race.

He finished seventeenth and was disappointed. But his tough finish could not take away from what he had accomplished: For most of the race, this high school kid had outrun the pros on the Craftsman Series. And it was only his second Craftsman race ever.

"We miscalculated on the fuel mileage, but nonetheless, we had a great run," Kyle said. "I hope I gained some respect among the other drivers, and we showed these boys we're not here to play, but to run up front."[1]

The Sears 175 was one of five Craftsman Truck races that Busch drove in 2002. He was the youngest driver on the circuit and one of the youngest ever to compete in a NASCAR series.

Kyle handled the pressure of professional racing well. He finished three of the five Craftsman races. His best finish came in the Orleans 350, when he was ninth. He made few mental errors and applied his aggressive driving style without any major problems.

His performance stunned much of the racing world, but it was no big deal to Kyle. His Craftsman Series experience was, to him, simply the next step in

THE 2001 SEARS CRAFTSMAN 175 RACE

What: NASCAR Craftsman Truck Series race
When: August 18, 2001
Where: Chicago Motor Speedway
Result: Scott Riggs won; Kyle Busch finished seventeenth

his progression into a pro driver. After spending much of his early childhood learning from watching his brother Kurt, Kyle Busch was ready to set out on his own.

He did. By the time he was eighteen he would have his own full-time NASCAR career going.

AN EARLY NASCAR START

Kurt Busch signed with the NASCAR team Roush Racing in 1999, and he made his debut on NASCAR's top Winston Cup Series in 2000. The next year he placed in the top five a surprising three times in his first full Cup season. His success, and the rumor that Kurt's little brother was the more talented driver, persuaded NASCAR teams to take an interest in Kyle.

"The reason I'm here, obviously, is because of my brother," Kyle recalled a couple years later. "He opened a lot of doors for me. . . . At the same time I wouldn't be (in NASCAR) if I couldn't hack it."[2]

Roush Racing had discovered Kurt at a tryout a few years

> **"The reason I'm here, obviously, is because of my brother. He opened a lot of doors for me. . . . At the same time I wouldn't be (in NASCAR) if I couldn't hack it."**
>
> —*Kyle Busch*

Kyle got his start in NASCAR's Craftsman Truck Series as a sixteen-year-old in 2001.

THE 2001 DAYTONA 500

What: NASCAR Winston Cup Series race

When: February 18, 2001

Where: Daytona International Speedway

Result: Michael Waltrip won

Note: Legendary driver Dale Earnhardt died following a crash late in the race.

earlier. In June 2001 the team invited Kyle to a similar tryout. Kyle was the fastest driver there, so he earned a test run at Chicagoland Speedway later that summer. He impressed the Roush team there, too. In late 2001 Roush offered to let Kyle drive in some Craftsman Series races. He seized the opportunity.

Kyle drove in most of the Craftsman races during the fall. He figured out a schedule that allowed him to travel to the races without missing much school. It helped that his teachers were understanding. Many let him come in early on Mondays to make up assignments.

"I'm an honor student," he said. "At no point did my desire to race interfere with my schoolwork."[3]

Roush Racing offered Kyle a permanent spot in the Craftsman Series for 2002. He really wanted to accept the position. But his parents insisted that he earn his high school diploma first. So while many of his friends were focusing on other things, Kyle was tuned into racing and schoolwork only. He wanted to get ahead.

Kyle applied himself and got on course to graduate from high school a year early. Everything was set for him to become a pro driver at age seventeen.

A ROADBLOCK

By 2001 NASCAR was exploding in popularity. The sport faced intense national media and public scrutiny for the first time in its history. The year also featured a devastating wreck that forever changed the sport. Legendary driver Dale Earnhardt crashed in the Daytona 500 that February. He later died.

An investigation revealed that Earnhardt's car had not been in very safe condition. Neither were cars that many other drivers used. They failed to take advantage of numerous technologies that could make their cars safer for racing.

WHAT IS THE AUTOMOBILE RACING CLUB OF AMERICA?

Founded in 1953, it's a national racing tour of stock car and truck circuits, featuring pro and amateur drivers. Its Web site is www.arcaracing.com.

NASCAR was embarrassed by the reports. The sport became obsessed with safety. One way that NASCAR addressed the sport's dangers was to institute a new rule: Nobody under eighteen could race. The organization thought younger drivers would not be as cautious as they needed to be.

Kyle was only sixteen when NASCAR announced the rule. He had already competed in six NASCAR Truck Series races. But that did not matter. Because of the rule, he could not compete in another NASCAR race until he turned eighteen.

Kyle was upset about the rule. "That was pretty devastating for him, for our entire family," Kurt Busch said. "Here he was ready to go, he'd done everything he needed to race full-time, and then NASCAR said he couldn't. We hoped he could get grandfathered in, but he wasn't allowed to race and it was a difficult pill for him to swallow."[4]

As much as the new rule upset the Busch family, Kurt said that it would not be a major setback in Kyle's career. "It was kind of upsetting, but that's life," Kurt said. "That's the bounce it takes and you got to work around it. And, the kid is only sixteen. He's got nothing but time."[5]

PATIENCE AND MORE WINNING

Kyle worked around the new NASCAR rule and moved on with his racing career. He spent the next

DURANGO HIGH SCHOOL

What: A public school in the Clark County district
Location: Las Vegas, Nevada
Nickname: Trailblazers

two years competing in ASA and Automobile Racing Club of America (ARCA) races.

Kyle graduated from high school in 2002. Now he could concentrate on racing full-time. He soon moved to Hicksville, Ohio, where his ASA team was based. In 2002, he placed eighth in the ASA standings, with four top-five finishes in the twenty-race season. The next year he won two ARCA races.

On May 2, 2003, Kyle turned eighteen. He was finally eligible to return to NASCAR racing. "It's been a long time coming," he said. "Ever since I got kicked out of trucks I have been counting down the days until my birthday. Now that it's finally here, I couldn't be more excited."[6]

Many teams were interested in signing Kyle to race for them. Most people expected him to sign with Roush Racing and join brother Kurt on that team. Kyle instead signed with Hendrick Motorsports. He wanted to mark out his own career away from his brother's shadow.

"Everything Kurt has ever driven, I've followed his steps right into that car," Kyle said. "It was kind of like Kurt was leading my way and I was going to follow him up into a Roush Cup car. I need to be my own person and make my own way and show everybody that I can drive."[7]

Rick Hendrick planned to enter Kyle in a few races on NASCAR's Busch Series, now called the Nationwide Series, in late 2003. Kyle was still only a teenager, but he was poised to race with veteran drivers on NASCAR's second-toughest national series. Hendrick thought Kyle had the maturity and talent to hold his own.

"Kyle drives like he's twenty-eight, not eighteen," Hendrick said. "I'm glad I got him because when it comes to racing, he's as good as anybody I've seen at his age."[8]

Others in NASCAR agreed. "Many of the heavies in the sport have already anointed him as the next

Rick Hendrick believed Kyle was ready for big-time racing when he was still a teenager.

NASCAR superstar," *Sports Illustrated* wrote in September 2003.[9]

Kyle thought he was ready. He was not at all intimidated. He had been preparing for a career as a pro driver for years. "This isn't short track racing anymore; it's the big time," Kyle said. "It's my job on the race track and it's what I am here to do. I'm here to try and win races and have the best time I can."[10]

He would both win races and have some fun.

4

MOVING UP IN THE RANKS

The UAW-DaimlerChrysler 400 race fell early on the Nextel Cup Series schedule in 2004. Kurt Busch was one of the favorites to win it, which had him excited. He also had another reason to be juiced about the March 7 race: For the first time in his pro career, he would be competing against Kyle.

To top that off, the Busch brothers would be driving against each other in their hometown of Las Vegas, at the Las Vegas International Speedway they had visited so many times as kids. They were thrilled.

"It's truly a special day," Kurt Busch said. "To have him in this series, it's truly an honor to have a significant note in the history books with two brothers racing in the same race. And here it is at Vegas, our home track."[1]

Kyle Busch made his Cup series debut at the UAW-DaimlerChrysler 400 in 2004.

Kyle Busch was also excited. Besides racing against his brother, he had another motivation: The DaimlerChrysler 400 would be the nineteen-year-old's first Cup series race.

"We're in the show solidly and that's all that counts," he said. "To come out here and run with Kurt and everybody else will be a lot of fun. . . . Hopefully, we can run up near the front where [Kurt's] going to be, and try to at least get some pictures out of the deal if not anything else. We're definitely going to have a great time running against each other."[2]

Kyle was not able to challenge Kurt. He struggled in the race, but the result was not very important. The DaimlerChrysler 400 was one of seven races that Kyle drove in on NASCAR's top circuit in 2004. After making a few token early appearances, Kyle competed in the final five Nextel races of the year. He was racing with the big boys, and he was still only a teenager.

That Cup series stretch was the culmination of a solid start to Kyle's NASCAR career. After competing in a few Busch Series races at the end of the 2003 season, he enjoyed a stellar full Busch season in 2004. He was so good that his Hendrick Motorsports team felt comfortable slotting him into the Cup series races.

Throughout 2003 and 2004, Kyle showed he could handle the pressure of being a pro driver. He met his own expectations and those of his team.

THE BUSCH SERIES

After signing with Hendrick and becoming a full-time pro in 2003, Busch competed in seven Busch Series races that year. His first was the Carquest 300 on May 24, at Lowe's Motor Speedway in Charlotte, North Carolina. Busch had joined new teammates in the middle of the season and had little experience. So he was not expected to do well. Yet he did. He finished second in the race behind Matt Kenseth.

Both Kenseth and Hendrick were impressed. "Kyle was driving the wheels off that thing," Kenseth said after the race. "He did a great job today and reminds me of his older brother."

"It's hard to be disappointed," Hendrick remarked about Kyle's second-place finish.[3]

Busch capitalized on the momentum of that start. He finished five of his seven Busch races that season. He came in second again at the Winn-Dixie 200 and seventh in the Target House 200. He was not surprised at how well he did. He had the talent and strong support from a Hendrick team that included Winston Cup drivers Jeff Gordon, Jimmie Johnson, Terry Labonte, and Joe Nemechek.

"I have such great resources," he said. "I can walk right up to Jeff, Jimmie, Terry, or Joe and ask them any questions I want and they'll answer them for me. That's not easy to find."[4]

Busch was excited, but he knew he still had a lot of maturing to do as a driver. For one, he needed to develop some patience. He had trouble accepting bad races. He often tried to force his way to the front even if he was risking a crash. In 2003 he failed to finish two of the seven Busch races he entered.

MATT KENSETH FILE

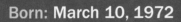

Born: **March 10, 1972**

Hometown: **Cambridge, Wisconsin**

NASCAR racing highlights: **Won Winston Cup title in 2003; placed in top ten of Cup series every season from 2004–2007**

Manufacturer: **Ford**

Sponsor: **DEWALT**

Team: **Roush Fenway Racing**

Busch worked on fixing that deficiency. "You have to get laps in and learn all those little things," he said. "Finishing is much better than wrecking, and that's a problem. Every time I try to get a top-ten [finish], I end up getting in trouble."[5]

Busch entered the 2004 Busch Series season more confident than he had been the year before. He already had a full offseason to work with his new teammates and could build on the experience he got in 2003. He would also get his own car for the first time in his NASCAR career. As the 2004

> **"Finishing is much better than wrecking, and that's a problem. Every time I try to get a top-ten [finish], I end up getting in trouble."**
>
> —Kyle Busch

JEFF GORDON FILE

Born: **August 4, 1971**

Hometown: **Vallejo, California**

NASCAR racing highlights: **Won Cup series titles in 1995, 1997, and 1998; finished in top ten of Cup series each year from 1999–2004 and 2006–2008**

Manufacturer: **Chevrolet**

Sponsor: **DuPont**

Team: **Hendrick Motorsports**

Web site: **www.jeffgordon.com**

KYLE'S 2003 BUSCH SERIES SEASON

Races: 7

Wins: 0

Top-ten finishes: 3

season started, he had high expectations. He was not the only one.

"At just eighteen, Kyle Busch is considered a can't-miss Busch Series champion," *AutoWeek* wrote on the eve of the season. "If not this year, then perhaps in 2005."[6]

Busch almost lived up to the expectations right away. He won five Busch races in 2004, earning 22 top-ten finishes in thirty-four races. He twice had streaks of at least six straight top-ten finishes. His five wins tied a series record for rookie drivers. In the end, Busch placed second in the series, behind Martin Trucx Jr.

As usual, Busch displayed a lot of driving talent in the series. Another key to his success was his patient, experienced teammates. They did not give him a hard time for racing with this patented aggression.

"Busch has found his entire team to be support-ive," the *Milwaukee Journal-Sentinel* wrote in June.

JIMMIE JOHNSON FILE

Born: September 17, 1975

Hometown: El Cajon, California

NASCAR racing highlights: Won Cup titles in 2006, 2007, and 2008; finished in top five of Cup series each year from 2002–2005

Manufacturer: Chevrolet

Sponsor: Lowe's/Kobalt Tools

Team: Hendrick Motorsports

"He's wrecked three Busch cars and two Cup cars and scuffed plenty of others, but every mechanic back at the shop understands that with a rookie driver testing his limits, accidents are part of the game."

Said Lance McGrew, Busch's crew chief, of the driver's reckless driving: "I've seen it before with guys that have been racing a lot longer than Kyle."[7]

Having such teammates helped Busch relax and focus on driving. "There's not a lot of pressure on me," he said. "I just go out there and do what we need to do every weekend and the team gives me what I need."[8]

ON TO THE NEXTEL CUP SERIES

By 2004, the Hendrick team thought that Busch was again ready to move up a class. They planned for him to join the Nextel Cup circuit full-time in 2005.

Busch celebrates his victory at the 2004 Carquest Auto Parts 300.

So they figured it would help Busch to drive in a few Cup races in 2004.

Busch of course wanted to win those races. But winning was not too important. The goal was to learn what it was like to compete at NASCAR's highest level—not to figure out how to place in the top ten, or to win. He tried to pursue that modest goal.

"Our goal, pretty much, is to try and go out there and make every race," he said. "Then, just to try and make every lap. I mean, if I can do that, it would be awesome for me just because the series is so darn tough."[9]

Busch showed up for nine Cup races in 2004. He qualified for six of them. In the end he finished both the Pop Secret 500 and Coca-Cola 600, placing twenty-fourth and thirty-second, respectively.

It was a good experience. Busch immediately noticed a difference between driving in the Nextel

KYLE'S 2004 BUSCH SERIES SEASON

Races: **34**

Wins: **5**

Top-ten finishes: **22**

Crew members douse Busch with sports drinks after he won the 2004 Cabela's 250.

Series and Busch Series. His car in the Cup series, for example, had 790 horsepower. His Busch Series car had only 660 horsepower. He had to adjust on the fly.

"It's quite different driving the two cars," he said. "The Busch car has a shorter wheelbase, less horsepower and more down force. The Cup car has been like an animal to me. It was so much more horsepower and with less down force, it's a bear to handle."[10]

Overall Busch was pleased with how he did in the Cup series in 2004. So was Hendrick. Now Busch was ready for an even tougher test: a full season on the series. Hendrick announced in mid-October that Busch would drive the team's No. 5 Kellogg's car in 2005.

Nobody knew how Busch's rookie season would turn out. But everyone knew one thing: It was bound to be interesting.

AN EMERGING STAR

Kyle Busch has been called fearless, brave, and even crazy. He is known for being an aggressive driver. He is often hell-bent on winning a race, or at least placing in the top ten. Sometimes he succeeds. Sometimes his aggression gets him into trouble.

"Skinny as a camshaft, Busch is all muscle on the track, driving with a passion that carries him to racing's ragged edge," the *Charlotte Observer* wrote. "Whether tucked into his car or hidden behind his wraparound shades, Busch races one way—to win."[1]

Long-time NASCAR observers say Busch is among a rare breed of drivers, those with supreme natural talent. He has the ability to control a stock

DALE EARNHARDT JR. FILE

Born: October 10, 1974

Hometown: Kannapolis, North Carolina

NASCAR racing highlights: Placed career-best third in 2003 Winston Cup standings; placed fifth in both 2004 and 2006 Cup standings

Manufacturer: Chevrolet

Sponsor: National Guard/AMP Energy

Team: Hendrick Motorsports

Web site: www.dalejr.com

car at top speeds. For example, he once won a Craftsman Truck Series race by driving the last several laps with one hand. He had to hold up an unhooked window net with the other hand.

Busch has been compared to past standout drivers such as Tim Richmond and Dale Earnhardt. Even Dale Earnhardt, Jr., who does not get along well with Busch, has spoken of the similarities between his father, Dale Earnhardt, and Busch.

"He's fast. He's running well. He's quick. He's aggressive," Earnhardt, Jr. said. "This is Dale Earnhardt in [19]89 and earlier. Daddy quit doing that stuff after a while, you know. But that's the way Dad raced, and Kyle has that same style."[2]

Busch's aggressive racing style is compared to that of the late Dale Earnhardt.

Busch has an intense love for driving, and it shows. He has competed in all three NASCAR circuits in one weekend, sometimes traveling to different cities to do so. He will race almost anything, anytime, anywhere. And he is very knowledgeable about cars.

"With Kyle, it's all about his passion for racing," said J. D. Gibbs, who runs Joe Gibbs Racing, which signed Kyle in 2007. "He says all the time, 'I love to race. Let's just go race as much as we can.'"[3]

Busch can race all the time because he is young, restless, and loves what he does. It also helps that he does not have a family to take care of.

"As far as me getting drained physically or anything like that, I don't feel like that's a possibility," he said. "I'm a guy always on the go. Even if I'm not doing anything that day, I'll go work on my Late Models, go to the lake, do wakeboarding, keep myself busy."[4]

Teammates like working with Busch because he works hard and is straightforward with them. These traits have earned him respect from competitors, too.

"Every crew chief wants somebody that's going to drive the wheels off the car. He doesn't go out there and half-ass it," says Rick Pigeon, who works on Earnhardt, Jr.'s crew. "If you make a change, he's going to tell you exactly what that change did and he's going to tell you if he likes it or doesn't.

"Some guys go out there and go, 'Yes, it's this and that.' For him it's, '[Heck] no, I don't like it.' That's why everybody [on crews] likes him. He gets 100 percent out of the car every time."[5]

TOUGH CONSEQUENCES

When you drive aggressively and try very hard to win every race, you are bound to have some scraps with other drivers. Busch has had his share throughout his NASCAR career.

In 2006 alone he was involved in multiple incidents with Tony Stewart and Casey Mears. He battled with Stewart twice during races that year. Stewart was furious. He accused Busch of being reckless.

"Kyle Busch, he's the one guy that's probably going to hurt somebody out here," Stewart said. "He's all over the place. He's what we like to call a bird with no feathers. He just doesn't know where he's going. . . . He just needs to learn how to drive."[6]

Many people disagreed with Stewart, saying he was as much at fault for the incident as Busch was.

The incidents with Mears, however, were mostly Busch's fault. They illustrated how he sometimes

TONY STEWART FILE

Born: May 20, 1971

Hometown: Columbus, Indiana

NASCAR racing highlights: Won Cup series titles in 2002 and 2005; was 1999 Winston Cup Rookie of the Year; placed in top ten of Cup series each year from 1999–2005

Manufacturer: Chevrolet

Sponsor: Office Depot/Old Spice

Team: Stewart-Haas Racing

Web site: www.tonystewart.com

CASEY MEARS FILE

Born: **March 12, 1978**

Hometown: **Bakersfield, California**

NASCAR racing highlights: **Won first Cup series race at Lowe's Motor Speedway in 2007; placed in career-best fourteenth in 2006 Nextel Cup standings**

Manufacturer: **Chevrolet**

Team: **Richard Childress Racing**

Web site: **www.mearsgang.com**

loses control of his emotions on the track. Busch and Mears collided during the Subway Fresh 500 at Phoenix International Raceway, and Busch's car spun out as a result. Another accident soon caused officials to unveil a red flag, giving Busch time to strike back. He hunted down Mears and bumped him, then drove off to his garage. A month later he threw a HANS safety device at Mears's car after a wreck in the Coca-Cola 600.

"It was hard racing between myself and Mears," Busch said. "I came down on him a little bit and we ended up cutting my left rear tire and I ended up spinning out. Before looking at the tape or realizing anything that had happened and totally taking the full incident into account, I took it under my own

Busch's car skids at the Coca-Cola 600 in 2006.

ambitions to retaliate—which is the wrong thing to do. I let my emotions get the best of me."[7]

NASCAR officials spoke to Busch after some of his mistakes. In one critical meeting, president Mike Helton addressed the Mears fights. Busch learned from those talks, he said. His actions are all part of maturing as a driver.

NASCAR insiders say Busch did mature. He began to drive with more caution and respect. So within a few years after joining the Nextel Cup circuit, Busch began to earn the acceptance of other drivers. "He drives really hard, but he's always driven me with respect," Jeff Burton says.

"Kyle's a hot shoe who drives the wheels off the car," added Rick Hendrick, who employed Busch with Hendrick Motorsports from 2003–2007. "He made some mistakes, ruffled some feathers. Guys want to see you pay your dues. He's worked hard to get that respect and I think he's got it."[8]

> "He made some mistakes, he ruffled some feathers. Guys want to see you pay your dues. He's worked hard to get that respect and I think he's got it."
>
> —Rick Hendrick

All respect aside, it is understandable why Kyle would be so aggressive and sometimes hasty on the track.

"For all those who are quick to point fingers at Kyle Busch and say he's out of control: Please keep an open mind," wrote *SI.com*. "After all, he landed a Nextel Cup ride with an established team at age nineteen. Combine his youth with his exuberance and he's bound to be cocky. He also feels the need—make that the pressure—to prove himself. Fast."[9]

KYLE THE VILLAIN

Although many drivers have come to respect and like Busch, the same cannot be said about thousands of NASCAR fans.

Busch is one of the most popular drivers in the Sprint Cup Series. He wins races and does so with flair and speed. But the attributes that make Kyle a great driver and a popular figure to some fans—his aggression and intense desire to win—also make him one of the most hated drivers in NASCAR.

Busch is often booed before and after races. He was even booed standing next to his mother, when he was introduced before a 2008 race on Mother's Day. Fans sometimes throw things at his car after he wins.

His unpopularity also stems from something that is not in Busch's control: He is the brother of Kurt Busch. When Kurt started racing in NASCAR, he developed a reputation as a hothead who won a lot of races but scrapped with other drivers, too. He got into it with some of NASCAR's most popular drivers, and many fans disliked him for it.

When Kyle Busch followed his brother into NASCAR, those same fans detested Kyle, too. In fact, he was booed before his first Busch race, when he was just an eighteen-year-old unknown.

"I've pretty much been doomed since I got here," he says. "I'm pretty much going to be doomed for the next ten years. That's why I just try to go out there and send [the fans] home unhappy."

"The poor kid," Kurt said. "He's got a bigger brother that did all the same things wrong, so he's going to get [criticized]."[10]

Kyle recognizes that both he and Kurt have made mistakes, but he contends that a lot of the criticism and booing is not justified.

Kyle was booed more than ever in 2008, when he won so many races. Since Kyle began winning a lot of races, now Kurt is booed because he is Kyle's brother.

Anger from fans intensified after a 2008 incident involving Kyle Busch and Dale Earnhardt, Jr., one of NASCAR's most popular drivers. Three laps remained in the Crown Royal Presents the Dan Lowry 400 in early May. Earnhardt had gone seventy-three Cup races without a win. He and Busch were jostling for the lead when their cars bumped, sending Earnhardt's car into the wall. Clint Bowyer ended up winning the race and Busch took second. Earnhardt finished fifteenth, extending his winless streak to seventy-four races.

KURT BUSCH FILE

Born: **August 4, 1978**

Hometown: **Las Vegas, Nevada**

NASCAR racing highlights: **Won 2004 Nextel Cup title; placed third in 2002 Cup standings**

Manufacturer: **Dodge**

Sponsor: **Miller Lite**

Team: **Penske Racing**

Web site: **www.kurtbusch.com**

Earnhardt fans were so incensed that Kyle had to be escorted from the track by security at Richmond International Raceway after the race.

The accident was not necessarily his fault, observers said. "Either one of those guys could have prevented that," said Steve Addington, Busch's crew chief. "It was just hard racing with a few laps to go."[11]

The heckling bothers Busch a bit, but he has learned to embrace it. When he was booed on Mother's Day, for example, he responded by raising his arms and cupping his ear. That only made fans boo more, but he laughed it off.

Like a young Dale Earnhardt Sr., Busch has become NASCAR's "bad guy." It's one of the sport's oldest traditions to have a driver become the "bad guy" for fans to root against. That guy is usually a driver who wins a lot of races, so it is not necessarily a bad thing to be the bad guy.

"He definitely has that personality that could be the villain," said Jeff Gordon, who was the villain when he won a lot in the late 1990s. "Sometimes he says things that don't always go over well, and sometimes on the racetrack, his aggressiveness can get him in trouble. But those same things allow him to have great success."[12]

Busch sometimes gets a good laugh out of all the hate from fans. He wishes fans would get to know him instead of blindly booing him, but he refuses to change his racing style or personality just to

2005 CHECKER AUTO PARTS 500

What: NASCAR Nextel Cup race
Where: Phoenix, Arizona
When: November 13, 2005
Result: Kyle Busch won

accommodate them. As long as his family, friends, and teammates appreciate him, he is OK, he says. Besides, he thinks the only way to stop the booing would be to stop winning.

"I've got a lot of people that support me, that really like being around me, and like being able to work for me," he said. "My team guys would run through hoops. They would run through fire for me. I've got the love that I need around me."[13]

The fans are fickle. During Busch's breakthrough 2008 season, many of them began supporting him. More fans than usual cheered him at races. His fan club membership surged. Perhaps Kyle Busch is not so hated after all.

KYLE AND KURT

Before the 2005 Checker Auto Parts 500, a NASCAR Cup race in Phoenix, Arizona, Kurt Busch was issued a traffic citation. His team, Roush

Racing, suspended him for the final two races of the season. They earlier had decided not to renew his contract.

Kurt was devastated. "It's tough," he said. "I'm a racecar driver. There's a race today and I'd like to be in the race. That's the decision they made and I'll have to live with it."[14]

Kyle Busch was in the race. He went out and promptly won it. Afterward he said he was dedicating his performance to his brother and the Busch family.

That race was indicative of the relationship Kyle and Kurt Busch have in NASCAR. They are on different teams but look out for each other.

Kyle (left) and Kurt Busch compete on different teams but stick up for each other.

Kyle is in a unique position as a driver because he is competing in the same circuit as his brother. It's common for NASCAR drivers to help teammates during races. But few have to worry about a brother who is not a teammate. Kyle and Kurt have always driven for different teams. But they still help each other. They stand up for each other. They also often share information about tracks, opponents, and racing strategies—even if they strive to beat each other.

"Kurt and I have a tremendous amount of respect for each other," Kyle says. "But there is always a sibling rivalry there, of course. The younger brother always wants to go out and outdo the older brother, so I've had that on me for a long time."[15]

Although they are nearly seven years apart in age, Kurt and Kyle had raced against each other before they got to NASCAR. In 1999, they competed in twelve legends car races at the Bullring near their Las Vegas home. They each won six races, with the other brother finishing second each time. The next year they raced a single time in legends cars at Irwindale. Kurt won the race and Kyle placed second.

BROTHERLY LOVE

"We don't really spend much time together but we do care for each other and we love each other to death," Kurt said. "Yet, we want to beat each other into the ground at the racetrack, seeing who's going to come out on top."

They have usually gotten along when they have raced each other. But not always. At the 2007 Sprint Cup All-Star race in Charlotte, North Carolina, Kyle tried to pass Kurt to the inside just three laps into the final leg. Both were in good position to win the race and the $1 million prize. Neither one did because they crashed.

They blamed each other for the accident. Kurt thought Kyle drove too aggressively. Kyle expected Kurt to allow him more room when he went for the pass.

Kyle and Kurt were both furious at each other. They did not talk to each other for a few days, until Kurt called Kyle. They remained angry at each other, barely speaking until Christmas. Kurt even publicly ripped into Kyle.

Then their grandmother asked them to come to a family Christmas celebration. Later that night Kyle and Kurt made up. They teamed up for a family board game and won.

"It was a little edgy to begin with because that was the first time we'd sat down together [since the crash]," Kyle said. "The more it kind of went, the more it kind of got back to friendly and normal."

Said Kurt: "Two brothers can make a mistake and blood is thicker than anything else out there."[16]

6

A SUCCESSFUL SEASON

Only ten laps remained in the Sony HD 500, a Nextel Cup race in Fontana, California, on the afternoon of September 4, 2005. Kyle Busch was leading the race, but debris on the track forced a caution. Busch needed to think fast.

He did. He made an unusual move. Busch showed that he was going to pit. That drew his competitors to follow him. But he only needed his crew to put on two tires, which they easily did. The quick pit stop allowed Busch to get back onto the track before every other driver.

"My nerves were getting to me," Busch said. "When I made that last pit stop, everybody followed me in and I thought, 'Cool, we're going to be all right.'"[1]

Busch was right. He held onto his lead and cruised home to win the race. It was his first victory on NASCAR's top series. After a pair of second-place finishes earlier in the 2005 season, he had finally broken through. He was thrilled.

"It's unbelievable," he said. "We should have been here at least five times this year, but we haven't been able to close the deal."[2]

It was a remarkable achievement. Not only had Busch won a Cup race, but the twenty-year-old set a record by becoming the youngest driver ever to do so.

Busch dedicated the victory to victims of Hurricane Katrina, a violent storm that had struck the Gulf Coast of the United States a week earlier. He promised to donate his share of the prize money for winning the race, and the share of car owner Rick Hendrick, to Katrina victims.

The Sony HD 500 was the highlight of a thrilling rookie season for Busch on the Nextel Cup circuit. He won two races, placed second three times, and earned 13 top-ten finishes. He was named the circuit's Rookie of the Year. He exceeded the expectations of his team and lived up to the hype that touted him as one of the next great NASCAR drivers.

2005 SONY HD 500

What: Nextel Cup race
Where: Fontana, California
When: September 4, 2005
Result: Kyle Busch won

Busch celebrates his 2005 Sony HD 500 win.

MODERATE EXPECTATIONS

After competing in seven Nextel Cup races in 2004, Busch looked forward to 2005, his first full season on NASCAR's top series. He had his own Cup car, his own team, and a bit of experience. He was prepared to race with the best.

He knew it would be a transitional, learning year. He would have to adjust to driving the larger Cup

DID YOU KNOW?

Before Kyle Busch won the 2005 Sony HD 500, Donald Thomas held the record for youngest driver to win a Cup race. He was four days older than Busch when he won in Atlanta in November 1952.

cars full-time. He tested one in Las Vegas and California and was pleased. He expected to be competitive on the series, even though not many rookies are.

Still, NASCAR observers predicted an inconsistent and difficult season for Busch. He was not used to losing races, and he likely would lose a lot in 2005. They wondered how he would handle it.

"There will be times when a victory looks a million years away, which is a feeling he didn't experience all that often in 2004," *ESPN.com* wrote. "How Busch deals with that adversity will go a long way in determining just how successful a season he has."[3]

Busch understood that he was entering the most competitive stock car series around and that he had to be patient.

"You want to go out there and win races, but to put it in perspective," he said. "You just can't go out there and expect to finish second or fifth or in the top five every week, or in the top ten every week. You've got to take your twentieth-place finishes and then once you finish there consistently then everybody says well then you've got to finish top fifteen, then ten, then five, and then you can win a race."[4]

> "Everybody says well . . . you've got to finish top-fifteen, then ten, then five, and then you can win a race."
>
> —Kyle Busch

But this was, after all, Kyle Busch, one of the fastest drivers in any circuit. So some observers predicted he would win a race or two in his rookie season. He thought so, too.

Busch got off to a decent start. He won the pole for the Auto Club 500, the season's second race, so he got to start the race on the front row. He posted a lap of 188 miles per hour (302.56 km/h), becoming the youngest driver to take a pole in NASCAR history.

But Busch finished only twenty-third in that race, after placing thirty-eighth in the season-opening Daytona 500. To that point, in nine career Cup races, he had yet to finish in the top twenty.

That would change soon. The next week Busch returned home to Las Vegas, Nevada, for the UAW-DaimlerChrysler 400. Many people predicted the hometown advantage would not help the inexperienced Busch much. In fact, oddsmakers picked him to be a 60–1 shot to win.

Busch did not win it, but he finished second. He nearly pulled out the race, challenging Jimmie Johnson until the end. Busch had started tenth and stayed in the top ten for the entire race. He was still in tenth place 180 laps into the race and then moved to seventh at lap 200. Twenty laps later, he moved to second.

"It was a lot of fun, and I hope it wasn't a fluke," he said. "I can't say it's bigger than any of my Busch Series victories, but it's up there. Everybody says I'm not ready, but we go out and do the best we can. And if we wreck a couple of cars, win a couple of races . . . whatever."[5]

Kurt Busch, who finished third, was impressed with his brother. "He is really coming together quicker than I thought," Kurt said. "He was pretty stout and I am pretty proud of him. He competed with the best of the best. . . .

"I'm done giving him advice. He beat me fair and square," Kurt added. "I'm beside myself really

2005 UAW-DAIMLERCHRYSLER 400

What: Nextel Cup race
Where: Las Vegas, Nevada
When: March 13, 2005
Result: Jimmie Johnson won; Kyle Busch finished second

Busch jokes with fellow driver Kevin Harvick before the 2004 Pepsi 400.

because I didn't expect this from him so early, but I talked him up like he couldn't do any worse and he was really coming together quicker than I thought."[6]

Kyle Busch finished second again a couple months later, this time in the MBNA Race Points 400 at Dover International Speedway. He finished just ahead of veteran driver Mark Martin, who was impressed by how consistent and clean Kyle's driving was. "He looked like he'd been doing it for fifteen years," Martin said.[7]

KYLE'S 2005 NEXTEL CUP SEASON

Starts: **36**

Wins: **2**

Top-five finishes: **8**

A HERKY-JERKY ROAD

Busch's first full Cup season was not all smooth. He behaved like a rookie sometimes. After the Sirius Satellite Radio at The Glen on August 14, for example, he slammed into driver Anthony Lazzaro. Busch and Lazzaro had bumped late in the race, infuriating Busch. Lazzaro called Busch a punk. NASCAR fined Busch $10,000 and placed him on probation for the rest of the season.

But Busch rebounded. He won the Sony HD 500 three weeks later, leading for ninety-five laps. It was his first Cup win, and it happened in the thirty-first race of his career.

Busch struggled in the next three races, finishing thirty-third, forty-third, and thirty-third. A dozen races still remained in the season. He did not qualify for the Chase for the Nextel Cup, but his team understood how important the final races would be. They were building toward a Cup-contending team.

Winning another race and continuing to improve were important goals to reach.

"This is going to be our practice run for 2006," Busch said he told teammates. "Now, everybody seems to be working together and heading in the same direction."[8]

Indeed they were. On November 13, Kyle won the Checker Auto Parts 500. He passed leader Greg Biffle with twenty-eight laps left in the 312-lap race and then held on. He finished the season twentieth in the standings out of forty-three full-time drivers.

Throughout 2005, Busch also continued to race on the Busch Series. He competed in every race in both the Busch and Nextel circuits.

It was a busy season and a successful one. Busch had won two Cup races. He also established himself on NASCAR's toughest circuit, earning some respect from veteran drivers and displaying the driving talent that allowed him to advance to the Cup series at the age of twenty. Now expectations for the Kyle Busch team would rise. Could he handle it?

FINDING CONSISTENCY

The 2006 Chevy Rock & Roll 400 is one of the most memorable races in recent NASCAR history for many reasons. Coming into the Nextel Cup race, eleven drivers were tightly packed at the top of the series standings. Most of them needed a good performance just to make sure they would clinch a spot in the Chase for the Nextel Cup, which would include only the top ten.

In fact, defending Cup champion Tony Stewart was knocked out of the Chase when he placed a disappointing eighteenth in the race, held at Richmond International Raceway in Virginia.

The race was also notable for Kyle Busch. He led for most of the way and finished second. That secured Busch a spot in the Chase for the first time.

2006 CHEVY ROCK & ROLL 400

What: NASCAR Nextel Cup race
Where: Richmond, Virginia
When: September 9, 2006
Result: Kevin Harvick won; Kyle Busch finished second

It was only his second full season in the series, and yet he qualified to compete for a Cup title.

He gave credit to his team. "Our car was so awesome. We should have won that race," Busch said. "Overall, it was pretty much a dominant car."[1]

The Rock & Roll 400 was a fitting end to a stunning stretch of races for Busch in the heart of the 2006 season. He qualified for the Chase and then was arguably the circuit's best driver for a few months.

Although Busch did not drive well during the Chase, the 2006 season was a great experience for him. He established himself as a contender on the Cup series and began to display consistency and even showed some signs of maturity. It did not all come easily.

AN IMPROVED DRIVER

Busch was a different driver in 2006 than he had been in his rookie season of 2005. Most notably, he

Kevin Harvick holds off Busch for first place at the 2006 Chevy Rock & Roll 400.

was a more confident driver. That helped him race with more consistency. As a rookie he had learned how to race on the Cup circuit. Now he felt comfortable competing against the world's best stock car drivers. He also had spent a full year working with his crew and was more at ease dealing with them.

Whereas the 2005 season featured a lot of strong finishes and many poor finishes, in 2006 Busch was much more consistent. He started the season by placing in the top five in three of the first six races. After three subpar races, he earned three more top-ten finishes over the next four races.

He was tenth in the standings thirteen races into the season. That set the tone for a good year.

"We're a better team because we had last year together and Kyle is a better driver because he has learned what to do in certain situations," crew chief Alan Gustafson said early in the season. "And we got off to a good start. That's put us in a position to race like we want to, not like we have to."[2]

Busch proved that he understood how to approach the Cup series. He loved winning, but he knew it was not always essential. The goal was just to aim for solid finishes each week. If he was in position, then he could go for a win.

"Kyle has always been able to go fast, but he is learning points racing is different from going fast," rival driver Jimmie Johnson said. "He is learning when to push and when not to, when to be patient and when to be aggressive."[3]

Other drivers also recognized Busch's improvement. They were not surprised. They knew how much talent he had. They knew that sometimes drivers make such improvements between their first and second full seasons on the series.

CONFLICTS WITH VETERAN DRIVERS

Despite his improvements, in 2006 Busch still acted at times like the twenty-one-year-old he was. While drivers such as Johnson respected him, other veteran drivers still did not.

That lack of respect stemmed in part from several incidents on the track. Busch got into spats with Tony Stewart and Casey Mears. He was often called a malcontent. Although he clearly was a better driver

Busch's crew pushes him into the pit at the 2006 Dover 400.

than he had been as a rookie, he was more often criticized for his aggressive driving than the year before. Rival Dale Earnhardt, Jr. even called him wild and threatened him.

"In his second full season on the NASCAR Nextel Cup circuit, Kyle Busch has had to balance the excitement from the start of another statistically successful season with the disappointment of a growing reputation for being brash, impatient and, sometimes, hot-headed on the race track," said a story on *ESPN.com* in May. "The result has been many a day on which great runs were spoiled by harsh criticism."[4]

Busch disliked the criticism. He thought he was being targeted because many veteran drivers could not relate to him or did not want to get to know him. He also questioned if they were jealous of him enjoying success at such a young age.

Busch took the blame for the incident with Casey Mears and apologized for angering Tony Stewart in a few races. He understood that it would take some time for him to earn some of his rivals' respect.

"There have been some instances where I've put my car in situations where maybe I should have thought a little bit differently about," he said early in the season. "But that's any driver. It's all about trying to gain respect; that's something that's important to me. I hope I've done a great enough job on that. I'm only in the start of my second year, so there's still a little bit more to do."[5]

Other drivers empathized with Busch. His brother Kurt advised him on how to handle the criticism and pressure. Team owner Rick Hendrick also reached out to him. Hendrick said Busch's struggles were just part of learning how to be a pro driver.

KASEY KAHNE FILE

Born: April 10, 1980

Hometown: Enumclaw, Washington

NASCAR racing highlights: Finished eighth in 2006 Cup standings, winning six races; won two Cup races in 2008

Manufacturer: Dodge

Sponsor: Budweiser

Team: Richard Petty Motorsports

Web site: www.kaseykahne.com

Driver Kasey Kahne, only a few years older than Kyle, also spoke up for him. "It's incredibly hard to be a young driver out here with all these veterans," said Kahne, then twenty-six and in his third Nextel Cup season. "It's hard to figure out when to give and when to take, and it's difficult to get the respect of the older drivers. But Kyle will be fine. His skill level is as high as anyone's."[6]

A turning point for Busch might have been the incident with Mears. Afterward he met with Hendrick and Mike Helton, NASCAR's president. They talked about racing etiquette and how to balance life and a driving career. Busch did not get into another incident for the rest of the season.

WHO IS MIKE HELTON?

Helton became the NASCAR president in 2000 and was still the president in 2009. He was the former manager of Talladega Superspeedway in Alabama.

> **"I came away understanding that it's better to have friends out there on the track than enemies. . . . it'll help me win the war at the end."**
>
> *—Kyle Busch*

"After that lunch I did a lot of thinking and realized that there's more to life than winning races," Kyle said. "I came away understanding that it's better to have friends out there on the track than enemies. That might not help me win the battles each weekend, but maybe it'll help me win the war at the end. . . . Still, I'll get after it when I need to."[7]

BUSCH MAKES HIS MOVE

After his good start to the 2006 season, in the summer Busch made his move up the series standings. In July he placed second in the Pepsi 400 and third in the USG Sheetrock 400.

The next week at New Hampshire Motor Speedway he won his first race of the year. He was in seventh place in the Lenox 300 when he hit a restart. The cars in front of him were running out of fuel. One by one Busch passed them. He then took the lead with sixty-nine laps to go. He never lost that lead, holding off Denny Hamlin and Greg Biffle to the end. Overall Busch led for 101 of the race's final 135 laps.

The victory pushed him into fourth in the series standings, just eight races before the Chase was to start. He had been in twelfth place only three races before that, but three consecutive stellar finishes put him in an excellent position. He just needed to continue his steady driving in order to make his first Chase.

"Any little mistake could put us right back out of it," Busch said. "We know that we have to keep on doing what we've been doing and run our own race."[8]

Busch kept doing his thing. He finished second in the Sharpie 500 five weeks later, staying in fourth. Heading into the Chevy Rock & Roll 400, he was in fifth. Still, he led the eleventh-place driver, Kahne, by less than 100 points. He could not afford a slip-up.

There was none. A second-place finish in the Rock & Roll 400 clinched his spot in the Chase. Busch would start the ten-race stretch run at fourth in the standings. Not only that, he had tallied more points than any other driver over the previous ten races, earning eight top-ten finishes over that stretch. He had spent nine straight weeks in the top eight.

2006 LENNOX 300

What: NASCAR Nextel Cup race
Where: Loudon, New Hampshire
When: July 16, 2006
Result: Kyle Busch won

HIS FIRST CHASE

Busch was excited about competing in the Chase for the first time. After his torrid ten-race streak to make the Chase, he was confident he could contend for a title. Some media members predicted he would even win it.

But the Chase did not go as he had hoped. He did not win a single race. He did not even earn a top-five finish.

He started the Chase by placing thirty-eighth in the Sylvania 300 and fortieth in the Dover 400. He crashed twice in the latter race. Afterward he was despondent. He had essentially given up his hopes of winning a title, he said.

But Busch rebounded to earn three top-ten finishes in the next six races. After he had fallen to tenth in the Chase standings with his Sylvania and Dover disappointments, he rose to eighth with two races remaining. But he finished only thirty-eighth in both of those races, ending any hopes he had of a championship.

Despite his disappointing Chase performance, 2006 was a successful season for Busch. He became a more consistent driver, earned ten top-five finishes and finished tenth in the Cup standings. And of course, he qualified for the Chase at the age of twenty-one.

KYLE'S 2006 NEXTEL CUP SEASON

Starts: **36**

Wins: **1**

Top-five finishes: **10**

More importantly for Busch, in the summer and early fall he began to earn more respect from the media and other drivers—including Earnhardt, Jr.

"He's matured a lot," Earnhardt, Jr. said. "He's found his groove as far as attitude and personality. He's found his little area that is good for him. Nobody has any issues with him anymore. He doesn't have issues with people anymore.

"He's made an attempt to really gain respect and he's got a lot of confidence," Earnhardt, Jr. added. "He does have some arrogance to go along with it, but that makes a real racecar driver."[9]

Busch hoped his hot summertime stretch and newfound maturity would carry over to the 2007 season. But it would be a difficult season. A controversy sparked by Earnhardt, Jr. would provide another learning experience—and the first serious adversity Busch would have to overcome as a pro driver.

8

A TOUGH TRANSITION

The 2007 Nextel Cup season started well enough for Kyle Busch. On March 25, in only the year's fifth race, he earned his first victory.

Driving in the Food City 500, Busch started twentieth. He surged toward the front and on lap 484 passed leader Denny Hamlin on the outside. After a restart with only a few laps to go, Jeff Burton passed Jeff Gordon to move into second, behind only Busch. He was right on Busch's bumper on the final lap, but Busch outraced Burton to the checkered flag.

Busch led the race for only a combined 29 of 504 laps. But a strong finish to the race gave him the

Busch earned the checkered flag at the Food City 500.

THE 2007 FOOD CITY 500

What: NASCAR Nextel Cup race
Where: Bristol, Virginia
When: March 25, 2007
Result: Kyle Busch won

victory and catapulted him from fourteenth to sixth in the series standings.

The good times did not last long, though. Busch's contract to drive for Hendrick Motorsports was set to expire after the season. By midseason Busch and Hendrick were discussing a new deal to keep Busch with the team.

That deal never materialized. On April 15, Busch was in a tight race at Texas Motor Speedway. But he wrecked on lap 252 of the 334-lap Samsung 500. Busch was out of the race, he thought. He drove to the garage, left the car there, and exited the stadium. He went straight for the nearest airport to fly out of town.

While Busch was leaving, his teammates repaired his No. 5 Chevrolet car. The car was good enough to make a few more laps at the end of the race, but they could not find Busch. They searched for another driver to finish the race. Dale Earnhardt, Jr. was available. His car had been trashed in the same wreck that knocked out Busch. So Earnhardt jumped into Busch's car and drove a few laps for Busch.

Busch's teammates were furious that their driver had left the track. Busch said he had been given permission to leave and that the race was over for him. But Busch was angry at Earnhardt. Earnhardt said he had just volunteered to help out Rick Hendrick, whom he considered a friend.

No matter what really happened, one thing is clear: The Samsung 500 sparked a rift between Busch and the Hendrick outfit. It also linked Earnhardt and Hendrick for the first time.

Hendrick considered not re-signing Busch to drive for him. Later that season, by coincidence, Earnhardt experienced his own dispute with his team. The team was Dale Earnhardt Inc. (DEI), and was named after his father, Dale Earnhardt, Sr. Earnhardt decided to leave DEI and sign with another team.

In July Hendrick and Earnhardt agreed to a contract. Hendrick also decided that his organization

KYLE BUSCH VS. DALE EARNHARDT, JR., 2005–2007

Nextel Cup Starts: Busch 108; Earnhardt 108

Wins: Busch 4; Earnhardt 2

Runner-up finishes: Busch 8; Earnhardt 2

Top-fives: Busch 30; Earnhardt 24

Top-tens: Busch 51; Earnhardt 42

Dale Earnhardt, Jr. took Busch's spot on the Hendrick Motorsports team.

would not retain Busch. The move was more of a business decision than a racing move. Busch was a more successful driver than Earnhardt. But Earnhardt was more popular and got involved in fewer clashes with rival drivers than Busch did.

"Busch was essentially dumped by Hendrick Motorsports when the team decided to sign Earnhardt," the *New York Times* wrote. "It was a slap in the face to Busch, one of the most talented young drivers in the sport. But it was also perhaps a signal that Hendrick had tired of Busch's behavior."[1]

Busch had mixed feelings about Hendrick's decision. He was upset about being cast away, but he did not mind moving on to another team. After all, he was a bit of a misfit with his more conservative Hendrick teammates such as Jimmie Johnson and Jeff Gordon, he said.

"I felt like I was probably a little bit more rough-edged, the kid who didn't care about what his perception was or anything like that," he said. "I wear my hair messed up because I really don't care, I'd rather wear jeans or shorts with flip flops and a raggedy T-shirt and go hang out on the lake, go wakeboard and hang out with some different type of friends. Jeff [Gordon] and Jimmie [Johnson], they fit the Hendrick mold and I just never fell into that. They seemed to be kind of spit-shined and polished."[2]

Busch was now a free agent. He could sign with any racing team he wanted. Plenty of them were interested.

> ❝It was a slap in the face to Busch, one of the most talented young drivers in the sport. But it was also perhaps a signal that Hendrick had tired of Busch's behavior. ❞
>
> —*the* New York Times

A TOUGH TRANSITION

More than half a Nextel Cup season still remained after Hendrick's move, and Busch was in contention for a title. Yet he still had to work for Hendrick. Many people thought Busch would crumble or quit on his team. They figured handling a transition to another team would be too much for a twenty-two-year-old to deal with while competing on NASCAR's top circuit.

At first it looked like Busch would fall apart. He had problems with Hendrick and teammates. Even his own crew chief, Alan Gustafson, criticized him. Gustafson would not be going with Busch after the season, he said. Instead he would work with Earnhardt or one of Hendrick's other drivers. He was upset at how his relationship with Busch was going to end.

"It just never was as easy as it should have been with Kyle," Gustafson said. "It's really disappointing that it didn't work out because I had hoped to finish my career working with Kyle and winning championships with him. There shouldn't have been a story here, but a series of mistakes were made, and it's sad that it got to this point."[3]

Gustafson planned to continue working hard with Busch in 2007, but he questioned if the team could stay in contention. He was unsure how Busch would react and how the team would move on.

Things did not look good after the Pepsi 400 a few weeks later. Busch was racing Jamie McMurray at Daytona International Speedway late in the race when he expected Gordon to help him. Gordon did not help, and McMurray held off Busch. After the race Busch ripped into Gordon and the Hendrick organization.

"I'm the outsider looking in now," he said. "The bliss is over at Hendrick Motorsports for Kyle Busch."[4]

Busch hunkered down and prepared to go through the rest of the season without much support from the Hendrick organization. At least he could still count on his loyal crew, he said. They still had eighteen races to go and were eighth in the Cup standings. Busch was fueled by the chance to prove Hendrick had made a mistake by letting him go.

"I guess it's a situation you really don't want to have to go through, but you do," he said. "We'll get through it. We'll be fine. . . . We'll make the most of this situation, make it into the Chase and hopefully be able to challenge for the championship at the end of the year and beat them all out and say, 'I told you so.'"[5]

MAKING UP AND MOVING ON

Just when it seemed like Busch would freeze out Hendrick Motorsports, he showed another sign of maturity. He set up meetings with Hendrick and

Hendrick teammates and reconciled with them. He apologized for calling them out at Daytona. He said he should not have opened his mouth when he was upset and that he wanted to stay friends with them.

Busch's apology went over well. Even reporters called him classy for his actions. So did his teammates.

"I was real proud of what Kyle did," Gordon said. "It showed to me a lot of maturity and it took a big person to do what he did. I was really proud of him and it will make a huge difference for the way we race the rest of this season."[6]

> "I was really proud of him and it will make a huge difference for the way we race the rest of this season."
>
> —Jeff Gordon

Gordon was right. Busch raced as well as any driver over the next few months. He finished in the top ten in eight of twelve races. Busch, Johnson, and Gordon all qualified for the Chase.

Busch entered the Chase as one of the circuit's steadiest drivers. He was in eighth place. In twenty-six races overall, he had earned six top-five finishes and fourteen top-ten finishes.

"Lost in the squabbles with Hendrick teammates and the speculation over which team he would drive for in 2008 was Busch's remarkable consistency," *Sports Illustrated* wrote. "With his great talent,

Busch is a threat to win in every race and is on the brink of fulfilling his vast potential."[7]

"He's been committed to Hendrick Motorsports," Busch's teammate Johnson said. "He's been committed to this championship and has been working real hard at our team debriefs to explain what he's feeling and doing."[8]

Even Hendrick marveled at how well Busch drove throughout this trying season. "I don't know that I've ever seen a situation in my twenty-five years where, you know, a guy knew he was going somewhere else and has stayed focused and determined to do the best he can," Hendrick said. "It's been real impressive what he's done."[9]

Busch attributed his strong performance to letting go of his frustrations with Hendrick and the peace that came from apologizing to his teammates.

"I've just been a little bit calm, a little bit more cool and collected, and a little bit more relaxed, just being able to enjoy what's going on," Busch said. "It's been a learning experience. It's been something that's been different. But I'm still building on trying to make sure we finish out this year strong, and that we're able to compete for the championship. That's the ultimate goal right now."[10]

A BETTER CHASE

Busch was a bit closer to reaching that ultimate goal in 2007 than he had been in 2006. After he had started his initial Chase poorly, he got off to a great Chase start in 2007. He posted top-five finishes in both the Sylvania 300 and Dodge Dealers 400.

However, he finished only forty-first at the next race, the LifeLock 400, and thirty-sixth at the UAW-Ford 500 the following week.

Busch rebounded. He earned top-five finishes in three of the next four races. Although he did not win a title, he finished the season fifth in the standings. That was his best showing in his three full Cup seasons. Observers were impressed.

"In working with Kyle over the years, I've always seen a guy that wants to do good and wants to be a champion and wants to be a race winner and loved working for Hendrick Motorsports," Johnson said. "He's done a lot of growing and maturing. Unfortunately, he's done all of his growing in front of [the] camera and national media and has made some mistakes. But we're all seeing that progress."[11]

FINDING A NEW TEAM

After Hendrick let Busch go, Busch had to find a new team. Busch soon became a coveted driver. His rare combination of talent, youth, and experience made him a driver that teams could potentially build around.

"Of all the terms that describe Kyle Busch—talented, temperamental, youthfully exuberant—you can now add this: most coveted free agent in

NASCAR history," *Sports Illustrated* wrote. "Never before in the fifty-eight-year history of the series has so young a driver who's a proven winner been available on the open market."[12]

Landing Busch would be an even bigger deal than landing Earnhardt, many NASCAR insiders said. Busch had enjoyed more racing success, was younger and more talented, and was touted as a surefire future Cup champion. The fact that Busch had been involved in many disputes with other drivers and had criticized his own teammates earlier in 2007 did not discourage team owners from trying to sign him.

"Kyle's a really talented young driver, and I just think he'd be the future of any team he went to," said Richard Childress, owner of Richard Childress Racing. "I can name you eight or ten guys in here at [Kyle's] age that were a handful. He's learning. I'd say this [experience] has educated him a little more."[13]

JOE GIBBS RACING

History: Formed in 1991 by Joe Gibbs and Don Meredith

First driver: Dale Jarrett

Owner: Joe Gibbs

President: J. D. Gibbs

Sprint Cup drivers: Kyle Busch, Denny Hamlin, Joey Logano (who replaced Tony Stewart after the 2008 season)

Busch poses with his new No. 18 car for Joe Gibbs Racing.

Busch eventually accepted a three-year contract with Joe Gibbs Racing. He would drive the No. 18 car, replacing J. J. Yeley in 2008.

Busch was thrilled. Joe Gibbs Racing had a reputation for winning races. In sixteen seasons Gibbs drivers had combined to win 3 titles and 59 races on the Cup series. Gibbs's other Nextel Cup drivers were Tony Stewart and Denny Hamlin. Stewart had won two Cup championships. Hamlin, like Busch, was a young driver who had already enjoyed some success on the Cup series.

KYLE BUSCH VS. J. J. YELEY, 2005–2007

Yeley: 76 starts, 0 wins, 1 top-five finish, 6 top-ten finishes
Busch: 108 starts, 4 wins, 30 top-five finishes, 51 top-ten finishes

"I'm confident this is the right place for me," Busch said. "Hopefully, I'll be here for the rest of my career. . . . Now it's time to loosen up a little bit more and enjoy racing in the Nextel Cup Series instead of it being just a job."[14]

Some observers thought Joe Gibbs Racing was crazy to sign Busch when they already had Stewart. Stewart, like Busch, had a history of clashes with other drivers and a reputation for running his mouth. He had also had run-ins with Busch in the past. But president J. D. Gibbs was not worried.

"I think if you offered Denny Hamlin, Tony Stewart, and Kyle Busch to most guys out there, they'd do that at all costs to make that work," Gibbs said. "You're talking about three guys that can obviously perform on the track."[15]

It helped that Stewart and Hamlin recommended that Gibbs pursue Busch. It also helped that Hamlin and Busch were friends. Hamlin got along better with Busch than any other driver on the circuit, he said. The two often talked about cars.

DENNY HAMLIN FILE

Born: **November 18, 1980**

Sponsor: **FedEx**

Manufacturer: **Chevrolet**

Team: **Joe Gibbs Racing**

Car No.: **11**

Career Highlights: **In his rookie 2006 season, won twice and posted eight top-five finishes; in 2007, won once and qualified for the Chase for the Nextel Cup; in 2008, won twice and qualified for the Chase**

"Both Denny and Tony said, 'Look, I'm telling you, off the track and on the track, there's no one that has the talent this guy has,'" Gibbs said of Busch. "We think bringing him on board really gives us three guys that can win week in, week out."[16]

Adding Busch would certainly upgrade the Gibbs team. Busch had far more wins, top-five finishes, and top-ten finishes than Yeley, who had been on the series for almost as long as Busch.

Many observers argued that adding Busch would improve the Gibbs operation more than adding Earnhardt would help Hendrick. Since Busch joined the Cup series full-time in 2005, he had earned more wins, top-five finishes, and top-ten finishes than

Earnhardt. Busch was also a decade younger and had been driving Hendrick's third car, which meant he likely did not get the Hendrick team's best equipment. Earnhardt, meanwhile, had been driving DEI's top car.

The Hendrick team understood what a talented driver they would be losing. "I hate the fact we'll have to race against him," Rick Hendrick said. "He's that good, and he's going to get better."[17]

Said Johnson: "Kyle has shown how capable he is to go fast no matter what it is. Put him on a tricycle, and he's going to haul butt. I think he's going to make Tony and Denny drive harder and elevate the status of [Joe] Gibbs Racing on his own."[18]

Busch had improved as a driver in each of his three full seasons on the Cup series. But as he prepared to join a new team, some drivers and media members figured he would have to take a step back before he could improve. Others, however, picked him as a dark horse contender for the 2008 season.

"The new [mature] Busch could mean new trouble for the rest of the garage in 2008," *ESPN.com* wrote. "If he learns to harness his emotions he could become the dominant driver many believe he should be."[19]

GIVING BACK

During his short career as a NASCAR driver, Kyle Busch has already made a large impact in the community. Busch runs a few initiatives to help poor and disadvantaged kids through his own foundation, the Kyle Busch Foundation. He also often volunteers to assist other drivers with their charities.

Busch started the Kyle Busch Foundation in 2006 after he visited St. John's, a children's home near Grand Rapids, Michigan. During his visit there he realized how important it was for kids to have a safe place to live, where they could learn and be encouraged to chase their goals in life. Soon Busch decided to launch a charity that would raise money for five children's homes like St. John's.

WHAT IS THE KYLE BUSCH FOUNDATION?

The foundation is a charity Kyle Busch started to help less fortunate kids in the United States. It usually assists children's homes and other organizations that try to offer safe places for kids to live, learn, and grow.

THE FOUNDATION TAKES OFF

Busch's foundation has been busy ever since it started. Take all its activity in 2008, for example.

In May 2008 Busch threw a surprise party for the children and staff at Carolina Children's Center, which takes care of underprivileged kids in Concord, North Carolina. For the party, he rented a private track and party room at NASCAR SpeedPark, an amusement park in Concord. While there he signed autographs, posed for pictures, and answered the kids' questions about racing. He even did a little racing with the kids, and he issued "Kyle's Heroes" awards to two staff members to honor their longtime service to the center.

Busch later chartered a bus to take the Carolina Children's Center kids and staff to the All-Star race at Lowe's Motor Speedway in Concord.

Busch's foundation has also teamed up with the NASCAR Foundation to help in the community. The two charities supported an event to raise funds for Boys Town Nevada in early 2008 as part of the NASCAR Foundation's Track Walk. "I am proud to

Busch signs a fan's tire in 2004.

be able to help give something back to my hometown," Busch said of the event.[1]

In September 2008 the Busch and NASCAR foundations teamed up for ServiceNation Day of Action. They worked on cleaning up and renovating the facilities at Carolina Children's Center.

"The work that the Carolina Children's Center does is very important to me," Busch said. "I had the chance to visit with the kids at the Children's Center, so I know how much they appreciate the volunteers spending their time to help make it feel even more like home."[2]

WHAT IS THE NASCAR FOUNDATION?

The foundation is a charity launched by NASCAR in 2006 that supports other charities through drivers and others in NASCAR volunteering their time and making donations.

Other programs the Kyle Busch Foundation ran or contributed to in 2008 included Pajamas for Orphans and Kyle's Miles. In July the foundation launched a drive to collect 1,000 pairs of pajamas for orphaned children. It was a project co-run by the Motor Racing Outreach program.

Busch also started a drive to raise $100,000 for The Pedigree Foundation, which helps dogs find homes, through the Kyle's Miles program. He asked fans to donate up to $1 to that foundation for every mile he drove during the racing season.

OTHER CHARITY EFFORTS

Busch has also been active outside of his foundation. In October 2008 he visited the Church of God Children's Home in Concord for a pizza party. He signed autographs and talked with the kids.

WHAT IS THE PEDIGREE FOUNDATION?

It is a charity that helps dogs in shelters get adopted and provides funds for those shelters to take care of the dogs.

Busch is inducted into the California Speedway Walk of Fame in 2006.

In May 2008 Busch accompanied driver Tony Stewart in a press conference to promote the Prelude to the Dream race. This race raises money for Victory Junction Gang Camp, which focuses on enriching the lives of kids with chronic medical conditions or serious illnesses, in North Carolina. Busch then competed in the dirt-track Prelude race at Stewart's Eldora Speedway in Ohio.

Busch has also donated some of his own money to help people. In 2008 he was approaching the record for most wins on the Nationwide (formerly Busch) Series. He had nine victories, one less than Sam Ard earned in 1983. Ard, sixty-nine, was battling Alzheimer's and Parkinson's diseases. His family needed help paying his medical bills.

The Carolina Children's Center is a children's home in Concord, North Carolina, that houses dependent, neglected, abused, and troubled kids. It provides services for as many as fifty-seven kids ages six through twenty-one.

Busch promised to donate to Ard's cause if he tied the Nationwide record. On November 1, he won the O'Reilly Challenge at Texas Motor Speedway, notching his tenth win of the season. He gave $100,000 to Ard's family.

"Sam Ard is one of the pioneers of this [series], and to be tied with him at 10 wins is something that's pretty spectacular and really, really special to me," Busch said. "I'm going to try to help him out and see what I can do. It's not much, but it's something that can try to help."

It did help, said Jo Ard, Sam's wife. "Kyle doesn't know what he's done," she said. "He really, truly does not know what he's done to take the load and the pressure off of me."[3]

> **"Kyle doesn't know what he's done. He really, truly does not know what he's done to take the load and the pressure off of me.**"
>
> —Jo Ard

10

NEW BEGINNINGS

After driving for Hendrick Motorsports for all five of his pro seasons, Kyle Busch joined Joe Gibbs Racing in 2008. In addition to the usual preparation for a new season, he now had to adjust to a new crew and new teammates as well. The process unfolded with amazing ease.

Adding Busch excited his new teammates at Joe Gibbs Racing, but it also worried them. On one hand they had not won a race with the No. 18 car in a few years, and Busch had proved he could win races. On the other hand, they had heard rumors and stories about how difficult it was to work with Busch. Once the crew and Busch met each other, though, they got along instantly.

"The guys were a little bit nervous," said Steve Addington, Busch's new crew chief. "They just heard the stories. And mostly it was the media or some guys on other teams that say stuff about him like, 'He's a great racecar driver, but he doesn't get along with anybody.' That was way wrong. Once they met him and got to know him and his personality, it's been awesome."[1]

It helped that Busch made the effort to get to know the crew before the season. In December 2007 he attended a company Christmas party and introduced himself to everyone there.

Busch also tested a Gibbs car in Atlanta, Georgia, in October 2007, just before his Hendrick contract expired. He and the crew enjoyed solid chemistry. It was almost as if they had worked together before.

"He came in there, and for some reason, I can't put a finger on it, it just clicked," Addington said. "He ran seven laps and he said, 'Load it, we're pretty good.'"[2]

The easy transition to his new crew gave Busch confidence heading into the 2008 season. So did his move to a new team. He felt less constricted at Joe Gibbs Racing. His confidence carried over to his crew, who predicted a breakout season for the No. 18 car. With Tony Stewart and Denny Hamlin also on board, the Gibbs team could not wait for the start of the season.

A SOLID START

Busch got off to a good start. He placed fourth in the Sprint Cup season's opening race, the Daytona 500, and then fourth again the next week in the Auto Club 500. He also continued to run the Nationwide and Craftsman Truck circuits and was driving well on those series, too.

Back on the Sprint Cup Series, he placed eleventh in the UAW-Dodge 400. Then he earned his first win of the season.

Busch was in the mix of the Kobalt Tools 500 in Atlanta from the start. He led eight different times for a total of 173 laps in the 325-lap race. Carl Edwards was leading with fifty laps to go, but his engine faltered. Busch took advantage and seized the lead. He led the final forty laps of the race, holding off Stewart by two seconds to win.

The victory ended a 147-race winless streak for the No. 18 car and its crew. They were ecstatic.

THE 2008 KOBALT TOOLS 500

What: NASCAR Sprint Cup race
When: March 9, 2008
Where: Atlanta, Georgia
Result: Kyle Busch won

As Busch crossed the finish line, a Gibbs employee got on his radio and thanked him for snapping the streak.

The Kobalt win vaulted Busch into first in the series standings. Only four races into the Sprint Cup season, his decision to sign with Gibbs looked smart.

"There's a different vibe surrounding Busch now," *ESPN.com* wrote. "Busch-at-Gibbs feels right. A lot of that may be due to his scorching start in the No. 18. Some of it may be because he joins two other rascally types in Tony Stewart and Denny Hamlin. Whatever it is, it works."[3]

> **"There's a different vibe surrounding Busch now. Busch-at-Gibbs feels right."**
>
> *—ESPN.com*

Busch struggled in the next two races, finishing seventeenth and thirty-eighth. But he rebounded with consecutive top ten finishes. At that point, eight races into the season, Busch was in second in the standings. He soon would take over the top spot, and he would stay there for a long time.

AN INCREDIBLE MIDSEASON RUN

Busch's amazing 2008 Sprint Cup run began with the Aaron's 499 on April 27 at Talladega Super-speedway. He led for a few laps late, fell behind, but passed Jimmie Johnson and Michael Waltrip to take

Busch celebrates with Joe Gibbs (right) after winning the 2008 Aaron's 499.

the lead again in the 183rd lap. He was still ahead on the final lap when a twelve-car crash forced a caution. Officials ended the race and declared him the winner. It was his first ever Sprint Cup win on a restrictor-plate track.

Busch was thrilled. He gave a lot of credit to his crew. Team president J. D. Gibbs said Busch was also responsible. He had won over his crew already.

"At his first test with us last fall at Atlanta, we realized right away we had something special," Gibbs said. "The No. 18 team has had some tough years.

Right now, those guys on that team would run through a brick wall for Kyle."[4]

The next week Busch placed second in the Crown Royal Presents the Dan Lowry 400. That pushed him into first in the series standings, ten races into the season. Rival drivers and others said he was a serious contender for the championship. It was not because he was winning and placing high in races. It was because he was driving with so much control and precision.

"When you watch Jeff Gordon drive, Jeff Gordon goes really fast. But you don't see a whole lot there other than going fast," Mark Martin said. "You watch Kyle Busch drive and not only is he going fast, but you see he is taking your breath, too. I've been there before—when you are at the very, very top of your game. He's got car control and he is smart enough to be able to make it. He's not wrecking them and bringing them back on a roll back. He's putting it all together."[5]

> **"You watch Kyle Busch drive and not only is he going fast, but you see he is taking your breath, too."**
>
> —Mark Martin

Through twenty races on the three national NASCAR series to that point, Busch had earned six wins. He was enjoying the type of season that few drivers, if any, ever had.

DID YOU KNOW?

Kyle Busch won seven of fourteen races between April 27 and August 10 of 2008, five more than any other driver during that stretch (Kasey Kahne won twice).

Busch stayed hot. The next week he won the Dodge Challenger 500. Then he placed third in the Coca-Cola 600 and won the Best Buy 400. Incredibly, it was his fourth win in the season's first thirteen races.

An accident in the Pocono 500 the next week gave Busch a forty-third-place finish. Then he finished thirteenth in the LifeLock 400.

The next week was the Toyota/Save Mart 350. Busch continued to slump a bit, qualifying only thirtieth. But on race day he dominated, leading for 78 of 112 laps at Infineon Raceway. He captured his first road-course win on the Sprint Cup Series. That sent a message that perhaps Busch was suddenly reaching his high potential.

Busch followed up the Save Mart race by finishing twenty-fifth in the Lenox 301. That setback did not slow him down. He won both of the next two races, the Coke Zero 400 and LifeLock.com 400.

Busch held off Carl Edwards late to win the Coke Zero 400. His LifeLock.com 400 performance was especially significant. It was indicative of the type of season he was enjoying. His success was part luck, but mostly skill and guts. Jimmie Johnson passed Busch late in the race, prompting Busch to tell his crew he thought the race was over. But a caution with only two laps to go in the 267-lap race gave Busch a chance.

Addington and spotter Jeff Dickerson spoke to him on the radio, urging him to be aggressive and to attempt a pass of Johnson on the outside. Busch listened. Starting second on the restart, he went outside and passed Johnson to steal the race.

Busch had now won three of the last four races and seven of the season's nineteen races to that point. Addington thought their success was something else. He said the Busch team was enjoying a dream season. Busch was basking in the success.

"You know, you cherish these when you can get them, and definitely this year is one to cherish," Busch said. "I don't know how to put it, it's so different. After winning one or two races a year, this is something that's crazy. . . . Last year, you would see Jimmie coming with 100 laps to go or fifty laps to go and I would tell my team, 'Race over.' And I was pretty much always right," he added. "You have to stay humble and you have to stay hungry. Somehow it's paying off and working out."[6]

> **"You have to stay humble and you have to stay hungry. Somehow it's paying off and working out."**
>
> —Kyle Busch

ANOTHER WIN

Following the LifeLock.com 400, Busch struggled in the Allstate 400 (fifteenth place) and Sunoco Red Cross Pennsylvania 500 (thirty-sixth place) races. Again, he rebounded from disappointing races. The next week he won the Centurion Boats at The Glen. Busch's eighth win of the season had many drivers, current and former, praising him and his crew as the ones to beat.

"They're very strong right now," Jeff Gordon said. "It's everybody's goal out there to try to break that momentum that they have, especially as we get closer and closer to the Chase."

"He's driving the hell out of it," said David Pearson, who competed on the Cup series from 1974 to 1986 and, in 2009, was second on NASCAR's all-time wins list. "Most drivers today don't do that. They'll run hard at the start of the race, ride around for a while and try to pick it up at the end. He just runs hard all the time."[7]

After The Glen race, Busch finished second in both the 3M Performance 400 and Sharpie 500. Then he placed seventh in the Pepsi 500. He closed out the regular season by finishing fifteenth in the Chevy Rock & Roll 400. He easily qualified for the Chase. He would start it first in the standings.

Busch celebrates his victory in the 2008 O'Reilly Challenge in Fort Worth, Texas.

WINNING ON OTHER CIRCUITS, TOO

While Busch was busy dominating the Sprint Cup Series, he was also a top driver on the Craftsman and Nationwide circuits. He combined to win twenty-one races on the three national NASCAR series for the season. During one stretch he won three straight Nationwide races, on three different types of tracks.

"He's been the guy to beat in all three series all year long," driver Matt Kenseth said. "Everybody knew Kyle was really talented, and when you get him with a group of people where the mix is right, he's going to be pretty hard to beat."[8]

Competing in three different circuits, sometimes in the same weekend, was a lot of work. Over one weekend in June, for example, Busch rode in five airplanes, eight helicopters, and four police escorts so he could get to each race on time. He got only a few hours of sleep each night. He was willing to do all that traveling because he loved to race, he said.

But that schedule took a toll on Busch. He finished last in the Pocono 500 Sprint Cup race that June weekend. Afterward he decided to race the Nationwide Series only part-time.

ANOTHER CHASE

Busch was confident heading into the 2008 Chase for the Sprint Cup. He was competing in his third straight Chase and had been the dominant driver on the circuit that season. He also started the Chase with a seventy-point advantage because of his regular season performance. He was the favorite.

"After waiting all year for the kid to crack, Cup rivals now recognize that the championship is Busch's to lose," *Sports Illustrated* wrote. "In putting together a breakthrough season he has become the circuit's most complete driver, winning on road courses, super speedways and short tracks, as well as—most significantly—on the intermediate ovals that make up five of the Chase's ten races."[9]

> "In putting together a breakthrough season he has become the circuit's most complete driver . . ."
>
> —Sports Illustrated

But just as in 2006, Busch got off to an awful Chase start. He finished thirty-fourth in the opening race, the Sylvania 300. His car came apart early, then he spun out on lap No. 83 and collided with Jamie McMurray. He struggled to finish the race and was devastated by the result.

"You can imagine his level of disappointment," team owner Joe Gibbs said. "He raced all year to get [atop the standings], and he's really down. I know what kind of competitor he is, and you've got to come back and find a way to make it."[10]

The Busch car was in a deep hole already, but Addington promised they would not give up.

Starts: **36**

Wins: **8**

Top-five finishes: **17**

Top-ten finishes: **20**

He tried to boost Busch, reminding him that he was not expected even to make the Chase in his first year with Joe Gibbs Racing. Busch got back to work.

But the next week he wrecked and placed forty-third in the Camping World RV 400 presented by AAA. Then he finished twenty-eighth in the Camping World RV 400 presented by Coleman. He was last in the Chase after three of ten races.

"We're out of the title hunt," he said. "That's for sure."[11]

Despite the horrible Chase start, Busch promised to continue to race hard for the rest of the season. He rebounded by placing fifteenth in the Amp Energy 500 and fourth in the Bank of America 500. He rose to ninth in the Chase standings.

He finished twenty-ninth in the TUMS QuikPak 500, falling back to twelfth in the standings with only four Chase races left. But he placed fifth, sixth, and eighth in consecutive races. A decent showing at the season's final race, the Ford 400, pushed Busch to tenth in the final Chase standings.

Busch was not satisfied with his Chase perform-ance, but few blamed him for his struggles. Some noted he was still young and could not be expected to handle the pressure of the Chase as well as veterans such as Johnson or Gordon. Others thought Busch had been the victim of bad luck after having benefited from a lot of good luck earlier in the season.

PUTTING THE SEASON IN PERSPECTIVE

Tenth place was not the finish that Busch had hoped for going into the Chase. But his Chase struggles did not erase the amazing regular season he enjoyed or the progress he had made so early in his NASCAR career.

"Probably during the offseason we'll just look back on this season and say, 'Man, that was pretty phenomenal,'" Busch said.[12]

"Even he surely considers this year one glorious opportunity that frustratingly got away," *NASCAR.com* wrote. "But make no mistake about it—Busch's season, when viewed in its totality, has been nothing short of spectacular. And the lack of a Sprint Cup title does nothing to diminish that. He won in often impressive, sometimes spectacular fashion on an array of technical or unforgiving tracks."[13]

Busch's amazing 2008 regular season and quick transition to his new team gave him a lot of hope for the future. By 2008 he had begun to realize his potential. At only twenty-three, he had truly emerged as one of NASCAR's superstars.

CAREER STATISTICS

SPRINT CUP SERIES

Year	Rank	Starts	Wins
2004	52	6	0
2005	20	36	2
2006	10	36	1
2007	5	36	1
2008	10	36	8

Poles	Top 5	Top 10	Earnings	Points
0	0	0	$394,489	345
1	9	13	$4,185,240	3,753
1	10	18	$4,821,090	6,027
0	11	20	$6,685,520	6,293
2	17	21	$6,617,590	6,168

CAREER ACHIEVEMENTS

- Won eight races on the NASCAR Sprint Cup Series in 2008

- Qualified for the Chase for the Cup on NASCAR's top series in 2006, 2007, and 2008; finished fifth in the standings in 2007, tenth in 2008

- Named Rookie of the Year on NASCAR's Nextel Cup Series in 2005

- Won two races in his Cup rookie season, 2005

- Won five NASCAR Busch Series races in his rookie season, 2004

- Placed second in the Busch Series standings in his rookie season

FOR MORE INFORMATION

FURTHER READING

Leslie-Pelecky, Diandra. *The Physics of NASCAR*.
New York: Dutton, 2008.

Martin, Mark, and Beth Tuschak. *NASCAR for
Dummies*. Hoboken, N.J.: Wiley, 2005.

Payment, Simone. *Kyle Busch: NASCAR Driver*.
New York: Rosen Pub., 2009.

WEB LINKS

Kyle Busch official site:
http://www.kylebusch.com/

Kyle Busch Foundation:
http://www.kylebuschfoundation.org/

Kyle Busch's NASCAR.com page:
http://www.nascar.com/drivers/dps/kbusch01/cup/
index.html

CHAPTER NOTES

CHAPTER 1. BREAKOUT

1. The Associated Press and McClatchy Newspapers, "Kyle Busch rules as king of the road," *The Seattle Times*, August 11, 2008, <http://seattletimes.nwsource.com/cgi-bin/ PrintStory.pl?document_id=2008104771&zsection_id=2002990521 &slug=auto11&date=20080811> (November 17, 2008).

2. Ibid.

3. Mary Buckheit, "Page 2 swaps paint with NASCAR's Kyle Busch," *ESPN.com*, April 2, 2008, <http://sports.espn.go.com/espn/ print?id=3326019&type=story> (November 17, 2008).

4. Dave Caldwell, "Kyle Busch Tries to Give Brother's Shadow the Slip," *New York Times*, June 12, 2005, <http://query.nytimes.com/gst/ fullpage.html?res=9C06E0DB1E38F931A25755C0A9639C8B63> (November 17, 2008).

5. Terry Blount, "Blooming rivalry between Kyle Busch, Earnhardt is great for NASCAR," *ESPN.com*, May 6, 2008, <http://sports.espn.go .com/espn/print?id=3383555&type=Columnist&imagesPrint=off> (November 17, 2008).

6. David Poole, "No-title fate mars Busch's great year," *Charlotte Observer*, November 7, 2008, p. 10C.

7. Ibid.

8. Ron Green Jr., "Aggressive Busch evokes a bygone era," *Charlotte Observer*, May 25, 2008, p. 1A.

9. Tom Sorensen, "Kyle Busch win races, but not fans," *Charlotte Observer*, May 17, 2008, p. 1C.

CHAPTER 2. GROWING UP ON WHEELS

1. David Caraviello, "Busch boys know Vegas is more than just the Strip," *NASCAR.com*, March 1, 2008, <http://www.nascar.com/2008/ news/opinion/03/01/kbusch.kybusch.vegas.dcaraviello/index.html> (November 17, 2008).

2. Lars Anderson, "In It to Win It," *Sports Illustrated*, Vol. 105 No. 11, September 18, 2006, p. 66.

3. Joe Menzer, "Busch boys share crash blame, but opinions differ," *NASCAR.com*, May 24, 2007, <http://www.nascar.com/2007/news/headlines/cup/05/24/kbusch.kybusch.lowes/story_single.html#page 2> (November 17, 2008).

4. Alex Tresniowski, Michaele Ballard, "Two for the Road," *People*, April 11, 2005, p. 139.

5. Anderson, September 18, 2006, p. 66.

6. David Caraviello, "Man who would be champ," *NASCAR.com*, September 12, 2008, <http://www.nascar.com/2008/news/features/09/12/kybusch.villain.good.guy/index.html> (November 17, 2008).

7. Tresniowski, Ballard, April 11, 2005, p. 139.

CHAPTER 3. GETTING STARTED

1. Scott Merkin, "Las Vegas teen makes big splash," *Chicago Tribune*, August 19, 2001, p. 15.

2. Lars Anderson, "Generation NEXTEL," *Sports Illustrated Presents*, November 30, 2005, p. 74.

3. Jim Pedley, "Not-so sweet sixteen," *Kansas City Star*, February 17, 2002, p. I4.

4. The Associated Press, "Busch-leaguer," *SI.com*, May 1, 2003, <http://sportsillustrated.cnn.com/motorsports/news/2003/05/01/busch_debut_ap> (November 17, 2008).

5. Pedley, February 17, 2002, p. I4.

6. The Associated Press, May 1, 2003.

7. Ibid.

8. Lars Anderson, "Burning Busch," *Sports Illustrated*, September 1, 2003, p. Z7.

9. Ibid.

CHAPTER NOTES

10. Jim Utter, "New guy takes wheel," *Charlotte Observer*, February 12, 2004, p. 5C.

CHAPTER 4. MOVING UP IN THE RANKS

1. Jerry Bonkowski, "Brothers savoring the moment," *ESPN.com*, March 6, 2004, <http://sports.espn.go.com/espn/print?id=1752941&type=story> (November 17, 2008).

2. Jerry Bonkowski, "Prodigy eager for Cup debut," *ESPN.com*, March 3, 2004, <http://sports.espn.go.com/espn/print?id=1750018&type=story> (November 17, 2008).

3. Jim Utter, "Kenseth beats Kyle Busch, but finish creates uproar," *Charlotte Observer*, May 25, 2003, p. 14F.

4. Jim Utter, "Hendrick duo on fast track," *Charlotte Observer,* May 23, 2003, p.5C.

5. Gary Graves, "'Generation Nextel' drivers are raring to go," *USA Today*, August 29, 2003, p. 4E.

6. Al Pearce, "Will Busch win Busch," *AutoWeek*, February 16, 2004, p. 56.

7. Dave Kallmann, "Racing from the get-go," *Milwaukee Journal Sentinel*, June 24, 2004, p. 1C.

8. Ken Roberts, "Rookie's skill belies his age as he seeks Busch title," *St. Louis Post-Dispatch*, May 3, 2004, p. D1.

9. Jerry Bonkowski, "Prodigy eager for Cup debut," *ESPN.com*, March 3, 2004, <http://sports.espn.go.com/espn/print?id=1750018&type=story> (November 17, 2008).

10. Shav Glick, "Busch Is Riding on Family's Fast Track," *Los Angeles Times*, September 2, 2004, p. D3.

CHAPTER 5. AN EMERGING STAR

1. Ron Green Jr., "Aggressive Busch evokes a bygone era," *Charlotte Observer*, May 25, 2008, p. 1A.

2. Viv Bernstein, "Kyle Busch is being compared to an icon," *New York Times*, May 17, 2008, p. 3.

3. Jim Utter, "With victories in all three of NASCAR's top series, Kyle Busch is flourishing at Joe Gibbs Racing," *Charlotte Observer*, April 25, 2008, p. 12C.

4. Gray Graves, "Track tripleheader fails to faze Kyle Busch," *USA Today*, June 6, 2008, p. 9C.

5. David Newton, "Hard-driving Busch forming special bond with the fellas at Joe Gibbs Racing," *ESPN.com*, May 22, 2008, <http://sports.espn.go.com/espn/print?id=3408683&type=Columnist&imagesPrint=off> (November 17, 2008).

6. Tom Bowles, "Strange bedfellows," *SI.com*, Aug. 7, 2007, <http://sportsillustrated.cnn.com/2007/writers/tom_bowles/08/07/kylebusch.gibbs/> (November 17, 2008).

7. Rupen Fofaria, "The heat always seems to be on Kyle Busch," *ESPN.com*, May 13, 2006, <http://sports.espn.go.com/espn/print?id=2443822&type=story> (November 17, 2008).

8. Nate Ryan, "Kyle Busch learns from school of hard knocks," *USA Today*, March 27, 2007, p. 7C.

9. Lewis Franck, "Give the kid a break," *SI.com*, March 13, 2006, <http://sportsillustrated.cnn.com/2006/writers/lewis_franck/03/13/inside.nascar> (November 17, 2008).

10. Ibid.

11. Newton, May 22, 2008.

12. Green Jr., May 25, 2008, p. 1A.

13. Seth Livingstone, "Points leader won't change to assuage fans," *USA Today*, May 22, 2008, p. 10C.

14. Paul Giblin. "One Busch Is Suspended; Another Struts," *New York Times*, November 14, 2005, <http://query.nytimes.com/gst/fullpage.html?res=9D05E7DE103EF937A25752C1A9639C8B63> (September 2, 2009).

CHAPTER NOTES

15. Mark Aumann, "Busch brothers remain close yet competitive," *NASCAR.com*, February 1, 2007, <http://www.nascar.com/2007/news/headlines/cup/01/31/kbusch.kybusch.vegas/index.html> (November 17, 2008).

16. Green Jr., May 25, 2008, p. 1A.

CHAPTER 6. A SUCCESSFUL SEASON

1. Mike Harris, "Night of firsts for Kyle Busch; points race shuffles," *USA Today*, September 5, 2005 <http://www.usatoday.com/sports/motor/nascar/2005-09-05-california_x.htm> (September 2, 2009).

2. Ibid.

3. Mark Ashenfelter, "Real test for youngest Busch begins," *ESPN.com*, February 25, 2005, <http://sports.espn.go.com/espn/print?id=1999649&type=story> (November 17, 2008).

4. Ibid.

5. Al Pearce, "Bet on it," *AutoWeek*, March 21, 2005, p. 44.

6. Rupen Fofaria, "Busch brothers beat the odds in hometown duel," *ESPN.com*, March 13, 2005, <http://sports.espn.go.com/rpm/news/story?id=2012404> (November 17, 2008).

7. Dave Caldwell, "Kyle Busch Tries to Give Brother's Shadow the Slip," *New York Times*, June 12, 2005, <http://query.nytimes.com/gst/fullpage.html?res=9C06E0DB1E38F931A25755C0A9639C8B63> (November 17, 2008).

8. "Kyle Busch running away with rookie honors," *NBC Sports*, September 15, 2005, <http://nbcsports.msnbc.com/id/9341482/> (September 2, 2009).

CHAPTER 7. FINDING CONSISTENCY

1. Mike Chambers, "Race goes to the quick," *The Denver Post*, September 10, 2006, p. BB-01.

2. Al Pearce, "Cup's biggest surprise?" *AutoWeek*, August 21, 2006, p. 38.

3. Ibid.

4. Rupen Fofaria, "The heat always seems to be on Kyle Busch," *ESPN.com*, May 13, 2006, <http://sports.espn.go.com/espn/print?id=2443822&type=story> (November 17, 2008).

5. David Poole, "Brotherly competition," *Charlotte Observer*, March 10, 2006, p. 4C.

6. Lars Anderson, "In It to Win It," *Sports Illustrated*, Vol. 105 No. 11, September 18, 2006, p. 66.

7. Ibid.

8. David Poole, "Busch goes extra mile," *Charlotte Observer*, July 17, 2006, p. 1C.

9. David Newton, "Maturing Busch starting to turn jeers to cheers," *NASCAR.com*, September 2, 2006, <http://www.nascar.com/2006/news/headlines/cup/09/02/kybusch.walk.fame/index.html> (November 17, 2008).

CHAPTER 8. A TOUGH TRANSITION

1. Viv Bernstein, "Kyle Busch is being compared to an icon," *New York Times*, May 17, 2008, p. 3.

2. Raygan Swan, "The 'Real' Kyle Busch," *NASCAR.com*, August 14, 2007, <http://www.nascar.com/2007/news/headlines/cup/08/14/kybusch.gibbs.q.a/story_single.html#page2> (November 17, 2008).

3. Lars Anderson, "NASCAR," *Sports Illustrated*, Vol. 107 No. 3, July 23, 2007, p. 70.

4. A. J. Perez, "Kyle Busch blames close loss on team," *USA Today*, July 9, 2007, p. 9C.

5. Mark Aumann, "Busch is poised in defeat, but sees writing on wall," *NASCAR.com*, July 9, 2007, <http://www.nascar.com/2007/news/opinion/07/08/aumann.opinion.kybusch/index.html> (November 17, 2008).

CHAPTER NOTES

6. David Newton, "Kyle Busch's apology to Hendrick teammates a class act," *ESPN.com*, July 30, 2007, <http://sports.espn.go.com/espn/print?id=2954501&type=story> (November 17, 2008).

7. Mark Beech, "Scouting Reports," *Sports Illustrated*, Vol. 107 No. 11, September 17, 2007, p. 77.

8. Dave Caldwell, "Kyle Busch Is Taking on the Present and the Future in His Bid for a Title," *New York Times*, September 23, 2007, p. 5.

9. David Newton, "Kyle Busch's maturity a new gain for Hendrick now, Gibbs later," *NASCAR.com*, October 15, 2007, <http://sports.espn.go.com/espn/print?id=3064533&type=story> (November 17, 2008).

10. Caldwell, September 23, 2007, p. 5.

11. Gary Graves, "Aiming to give team top Chase positions," *USA Today*, November 8, 2007, p. 10C.

12. Anderson, July 23, 2007, p. 70.

13. J. P. Vettraino, "He'll be back," *AutoWeek*, June 25, 2007, p. 70.

14. Jeff Wolf, "Busch excited about change," *Las Vegas Review-Journal*, August 15, 2007, p. 1C.

15. Joe Menzer, "Busch's character another piece to the Gibbs puzzle," *NASCAR.com*, n.d. <http://www.nascar.com/2007/news/opinion/08/14/jmenzer.kybusch.gibbs/story_single.html#page2> (November 17, 2008).

16. Jeff Wolf, "Busch excited about change," *Las Vegas Review-Journal*, August 15, 2007, p. 1C.

17. Graves, November 8, 2007, p. 10C.

18. Nate Ryan, "Kyle Busch shows versatility, tops two series," *USA Today*, February 26, 2008, p. 9C.

19. Newton, Oct. 15, 2007,

CHAPTER 9. GIVING BACK

1. "Kyle Busch joins efforts to walk for charity in Vegas," *NASCAR.com*, January 29, 2008, <http://www.nascar.com/2008/news/headlines/official/01/29/nascar.foundation.track.walk.kbusch/index.html> (November 17, 2008).

2. "The NASCAR Foundation and Kyle Busch Foundation team up for the ServiceNation Day of Action on Sept. 27," *Kyle Busch Foundation's Web site*, September 24, 2008, <http://www.kylebuschfoundation.org> (November 17, 2008).

3. Jeff Wolf, "Leftovers," *Las Vegas Review-Journal*, November 4, 2008, p. 2C.

CHAPTER 10. NEW BEGINNINGS

1. David Newton, "Hard-driving Busch forming special bond with the fellas at Joe Gibbs Racing," *ESPN.com*, May 22, 2008, <http://sports.espn.go.com/espn/print?id=3408683&type=Columnist&imagesPrint=off> (November 17, 2008).

2. Ibid.

3. Marty Smith, "Kyle Busch, the forgotten man in Junior swap, doing just fine, thank you," *ESPN.com*, February 27, 2008, <http://sports.espn.go.com/espn/print?id=3266891&type=story> (November 17, 2008).

4. Jim Utter, "With victories in all three of NASCAR's top series, Kyle Busch is flourishing at Joe Gibbs Racing," *Charlotte Observer*, April 25, 2008, p. 12C.

5. Bruce Martin, "Busch, Biffle set early pace for '08," *SI.com*, March 21, 2008, <http://sportsillustrated.cnn.com/2008/writers/bruce_martin/03/21/notes/index.html> (November 17, 2008).

6. David Poole, "Race fortunes breaking for Busch," *Charlotte Observer*, July 14, 2008, p. 1C.

CHAPTER NOTES

7. David Newton, "Kyle Busch on the kind of tear few drivers have known," *ESPN.com*, July 11, 2008, <http://sports.espn.go.com/rpm/nascar/cup/columns/story?columnist=newton_david&page=InsideTheHauler20080711> (November 17, 2008).

8. Nate Ryan, "Victorious Kyle Busch revels in bad-guy image," *USA Today*, May 12, 2008, p. 10C.

9. Mark Beech, "Scouting Report," *Sports Illustrated*, Vol. 109 No. 10, September 15, 2008, p. 77.

10. "Race report," *AutoWeek*, September 22, 2008, p. 0045.

11. David Poole, "Can he come back?" *Charlotte Observer*, September 28, 2008, p. 6C.

12. David Poole, "No-title fate mars Busch's great year," *Charlotte Observer*, November 7, 2008, p. 10C.

13. David Caraviello, "Lack of Cup title doesn't diminish Busch's season," *NASCAR.com*, November 5, 2008, <http://www.nascar.com/2008/news/opinion/11/05/inside.line.dcaraviello.kybusch.success/story_single.html#page2> (November 17, 2008).

GLOSSARY

Busch Series—The NASCAR series that was one notch below the Cup series. Renamed the Nationwide Series in 2008.

Chase for the Cup—Competition between the top ten drivers on the Cup series over the last ten races of the season.

crew chief—The person in charge of the driver's car; the crew chief talks with the driver and the rest of the driver's team during a race.

NASCAR—The National Association for Stock Car Auto Racing, the highest level of stock car racing.

Nationwide Series—The NASCAR series that is one notch below the Cup series. It was formerly called the Busch Series.

Nextel Cup—The award that was given annually to the winner of the Chase for the Cup from 2004–2007.

pit crew—The mechanics who work as a team to make adjustments to the car, such as changing tires, during a race.

pit road—The area where pit crews service the cars, usually along the front straightaway.

GLOSSARY

pole position—The leading position at the start of the race, awarded to the fastest driver during qualifying.

qualifying—A process in which cars are timed in laps on the track by themselves. The fastest cars get to start in the best positions for a race.

speedway—A track for car races.

sponsor—A business that pays money to a race team, generally in exchange for advertising, such as having its logo painted on the car.

Sprint Cup—The award given annually to the winner of the Chase for the Cup, as of 2008.

stock car—A standard type of automobile that is modified for use in racing.

Winston Cup—The award that was given annually to the winner of NASCAR's top series from 1971–2003.

INDEX

INDEX